EDUARDO M. GIL MARTÍNEZ

Spanish Air Force During World War II

Germany's Hidden Ally?

Dedicated to:
Solete (my life)
My parents Salud y Eduardo.
Merce, Caco y Ricardo.
Ángel y sus nietos June, Iñigo e Ibón.

Acknowledgments for their invaluable help in bringing this work to fruition: Juan Arráez Cerdá (without his help this text never come true), Marisol García Gómez (the inspiration), Ricardo Ramallo Gil, Nicole Mucha (for her kindness and effort), Juan Pérez Blanco (for his help in the graphic design), Fernando Salobral (from Almena), Guillermo Martín Pérez (the Expert man), Asisbiz, José Antonio Muñoz Molero, Aviationcorner.net, and Javier González, John Mellor, Pedro M. Moreno (generous Aviation lovers).

EDUARDO M. GIL MARTÍNEZ

Spanish Air Force During World War II

Germany's Hidden Ally?

KAGERO

FIRST EDITION
© by KAGERO Publishing, 2019

AUTHOR
Eduardo M. Gil Martínez

EDITORS
Eduardo M. Gil Martínez

TRANSLATION/PROOFREADING
Ricardo Ramallo Gil

COVER
Łukasz Maj

DTP
Kagero Studio, Jacek Sadowski

COLOR PROFILES
Color profiles: Arkadiusz Wróbel

PHOTO SOURCE
Juan Arráez archives, Almena Ediciones, Military Modeling and History, Aviationcorner.net,
Bundesarchiv, Rod's Warbirds, Luís E Togores, Asisbiz and Public Domain

LUBLIN 2019

ISBN 978-83-66148-17-8

DISTRIBUTION
Kagero Publishing
ul. Akacjowa 100, os. Borek, Turka, 20-258 Lublin 62, Poland
phone +48 601-602-056, phone/fax +48 81 501-21-05
e-mail: marketing@kagero.pl
www.kagero.pl

Index

Chapter VII

Chapter VIII

Chapter IX

Chapter X

Chapter XI

Chapter XII

Annexes

Introduction

In the same way as in my last books about Bulgarian Air Force and Aeronautica Nazionale Repubblicana during World War II (WW2), this book brings us the often unknown History of other Air Force not allied to Germany during World War II but that even fought together with the Luftwaffe against the USSR. We are talking about the Ejército del Aire español (EdA) or in English language Spanish Air Force. Spain had just finished the Spanish Civil War in 1939, just a few months before WW2 began. The winning side, led by Francisco Franco, had received the help of Germans and Italians, which proved decisive in winning the war. Although at first, it would have been logical to think that Spain joined Germany in WW2, the country was destroyed and exhausted after three years of fighting, so it was not belligerent. Despite this, the proximity to Germany and Italy was evident in Spanish foreign policy.

We will be able to know how, despite the Spanish non belligerence, there were many incidents with airplanes mainly of the Allies during the WW2. We will also rescue from oblivion the Escuadrillas Azules or in English language Blue Squadrons that were sent from Spain to fight manning German aircraft within the Luftwaffe against the USSR.

The EdA and the Blue Squadrons have been studied in a few cases in English, highlighting the "In the skies of Europe" from Hans Werner Neulen, or in French with Juan Arráez Cerdá works. Although fortunately this History in Spain is better known thanks to several works about the matter from authors as José Luis González Serrano (the superb "Las unidades y el material del Ejército del Aire durante la Segunda Guerra mundial"), Juan Arráez Cerdá (several excellent Works), Jorge Fernández-Coppel Larrinaga, Carlos Caballero Jurado, Francisco Martínez Canales or the Servicio Histórico del Ejército del Aire to name the main. We want to compile in a didactic way but without academic intention, the information about this topic from these authors that have been the basis of this text; but a search has been necessary in dozens of sources to try to complete the research and offer it in the most definite way.

It´s very important too, the great work of several webs and facebook that have the EdA as their matter of study and never forget the courage of its men (memoriablau, forosegundaguerra.com, Españoles en la Segunda Guerra mundial, etc).

So, thanks to a this research we have been able to create a text that brings us closer to know the little known history of the Ejército del Aire during World War II with its several branches; and to know the courage that the Spanish pilots and ground crews demonstrated in their struggle mainly against Soviet planes but Allies planes too.

Serve this text as a tribute and as a reminder of these valerous men that tried to defend their country from intruders more powerful than them and that send more than 50 volunteer pilots to fight against the USSR.

CHAPTER I

Spain During The World War 2

The book you have in your hands tries to recall the history of some of the Spaniards who fought in World War 2 (WW2) on the German side; completely lacking any political purpose.

The Spanish troops intervention during the Second World War within the German armed forces is fortunately better known in our country (Spain), thanks to the increasingly abundant works that have been appearing in last years. These works are mainly about the Spaniards integrated in the Wehrmacht, the well-known Blue Division and its successor Blue Legion; and to a lesser extent, about the Spaniards who joined the Kriegsmarine or the Luftwaffe or the irreducible ones who kept fighting alongside the Germans until the end of the war (I wrote a book about this unknown matter).

It is known that there were many Spaniards who fought for the Western Allies and for the Soviets, but in this text we will not study their history since they did not belong at that time to the Spanish Air Force and in the case of Aviation, they never acted in squadrons completely integrated by Spanish pilots, but mixed with pilots from different nations (as it happened with the Spaniards who fought in Soviet airplanes during the WW2). Although these pilots demonstrated the same courage and bravery as the EdA pilots, this text is not about their interesting story.

The Spanish situation that was decreed at the beginning of the world conflict in September 1939 was neutrality despite the fact that a good part of the Germanophile population existed in Spain; in that decree we can read that „knowing officially the state of war that unfortunately exists between England, France and Poland on one side, and Germany, on the other, is hereby ordered, the strictest neutrality to the Spanish citizen".

The geographical situation of Spain and the Moroccan Protectorate under Spanish control, with the consequent dominion of the Strait of Gibraltar, as well as the high strategic value of the Balearic Islands (in the Mediterranean) and the Canary Islands (in the Atlantic) motivated the start of national defense Plans from the High Command.

This Spanish interest to improve the national territory defense was not wrong, since the United Kingdom had set as a possible target the Canary Islands as we will see later. On the other hand, although the German Reich maintained an interest by these islands (within the project of a new German colonial empire), did not try to obtain them by the force but in exchange for territories conquered to France in northwestern Africa.

After the important Allies defeats against the German Army, on June 12, 1940 Spain went to "non-belligerency" situation, in a similar way to how Italy did before joining the world conflict. Despite the first step that Spain took towards Germany, the negotiations for the entry into the war carried out with Von Ribbentrop did not culminate in the union of Spain with the Axis due to lack of understanding (voluntary or not) on both sides.

The events were developing at great speed in Europe and on June 25, 1940 the armistice came in France. In October 1940 Hitler and Franco met in the French town of Hendaye with the intention that Spain would join Germany in the war (as happened with Mussolini in Bordighera in February 1941), but the Spanish demands prevented the pact. For this reason, the situation in which Spain was facing Germany was quite complex.

It is true, according to Neulen, that Spain was possibly the only country in which a large part of the population saw Germany's attack on the USSR with satisfaction. The Spanish Civil War (SCW) was very recent (it ended on April 1, 1939) and the USSR had helped the defeated side. The winning side (the Nationalists) under Francisco Franco command was clearly opposed to communism and of course to the country that was the communism symbol: the USSR.

The invasion of the Soviet Union decreased the pressure that Adolf Hitler performed on Francisco Franco, by means of the shipment of an expeditionary force to Russia. This step was considered by the Germans at the beginning as a first step for the gradual entry of Spain into the war. Also this troops shipment to integrate in the German Army, would allow them to "pay" indirectly part of the debt contracted by Spain with Germany in concept for the help of Germany in the SCW to the Nationalist band.

The movements carried out by Spain, very close to German interests, caused the Spanish territory and more specifically the Canary Islands to become a desired target for the British (at that time the French Vichy had refused to cede Casablanca to Germany, so the German interest of the Spanish islands also increased since the summer of 1940). The British interest (along with its Canadian allies) for the Canary Islands lasted at least until autumn of 1943, taking shape in the so-called Bugler, Chutney, Puma, Pilgrim and Tonic operations, whose purpose among others was the capture of strategic positions in the Canary Islands (especially on the island of Gran Canaria and its aerodrome located in Gando, as well as on Tenerife island) through which they could maintain air and maritime control over German submarines. The disembarkation would take place in the Gando Bay, advancing towards the north of the island until reaching Las Palmas. In June, 1941, Force 110 was formed in Inveray (Scotland), which had to take part in this plan and which should be about 25,000 men. The Force was composed of 3 Army brigades, 2 of the Marines and several artillery and armored support units.

It is a known fact, although most of the Spanish population is not familiar with it, the existence of the Spanish Volunteers Division, (popularly known as the Blue Division or División Azul) that emerged as a response to popular clamor on part of the Spanish population that after the German army attack to the USSR in June 1941, showed the desire to fight the Soviets in their own country with a large demonstration in Madrid guided mainly by the Spanish phalanx (Falange española). To return the visit they had made to support the Republican side during the Spanish Civil War, while they returned the favor and partly paid the debt owed to Germany for their support to the National side in that war. It was during this demonstration, when Serrano Suñer, Minister of Foreign Affairs and Chairman of the Falange Political Council, from one of the balconies of the General Secretariat of the Movement headquarters delivered his well-known speech:

"Comrades, it is not time for speeches; it is time that Falange dictates at this moment his condemnatory sentence: Russia is guilty! It is guilty of our Civil War. It is guilty of the death of José Antonio, our founder and of so many comrades and so many soldiers fallen in that war for the aggression of Russian communism. The extermination of Russia is a requirement of the history and future of Europe..."

Due to the great popular enthusiasm that was generated, little effort was necessary to recruit its members among the military and thousands of volunteers who prepared to sign their names in the recruitment offices that were created for that purpose. Among these volunteers, there were some soldiers who had not fought in the Spanish Civil War and wanted to prove to themselves and their comrades that they were capable of going to the front. It is said that some young officers fresh out of the Academy, faced with the war in the world, did not agree to let this opportunity that was presented to them pass by. Also in young university students with a desire for adventure, or with the romantic ideal of defending convictions such as God and Homeland, they strongly grasped the idea of enlisting in the Spanish Volunteers Division.

As an element of support to the Spanish ground forces, it was decided to also create an air unit to accompany them on the battle front. For this reason, an air component corresponding to a Fighter Squadron was created; officially called the Expeditionary Squadron in Russia and popularly known as the Blue Squadron (Escuadrilla Azul). We will see later how the Spanish infantry never received the support of their compatriots from the Blue Squadron, even though that was the intention of the Spanish Government.

In July 1941 a contingent of some 18,000 men under the command of General Agustín Muñoz Grandes (later to be relieved by General Emilio Esteban Infantes in December 1942), left to Germany to receive the appropriate instruction in Grafenwöhr training camp, then they were integrated within the German army with the denomination of Infanterie Division 250 (Infantry Division 250). Later and from September 29 in the same year they would fight integrated into the 16th German Army in Army Group North.

But German power over Europe began to decrease on the Russian front and in North Africa. In November of 1942 the operation "Torch" took place in which the British and Americans occupied the western Maghreb. The situation became very complicated for the Spanish Government, since the Canary Islands and the Spanish Protectorate in Morocco were at the mercy of the Western Allies. The USA began to be interested in the Canary Islands (until 1943 the interest had been small), which they want as a maritime surveillance post on the African Atlantic coast. In fact, there would be several clashes between planes and the Spanish anti-aircraft artillery and Allied aircraft during the next years.

Due to this situation, on December 12, 1942, General Muñoz Grandes received the order to return to Spain, despite the important opposition presented by the Germans to his departure. And two days later Adolf Hitler imposed the Oak Leaves on his Knight's Cross of the Iron Cross Order, which he already possessed. The command fell to the then second chief of the Division, General Emilio Esteban Infantes Martín, who would also receive the Knight's Cross of the Iron Cross later.

Spain repeatedly requested German war material, although with little success. It was not until 1943 that various German-made war armament could be purchased within the Bär Program. Regarding the issue that we are dealing with in this text, the Air Force, Spain received 15 Bf 109 F4 (originally Spain had requested at least 250), 10 Ju 88 A4, in addition to various appliances for air navigation (which will be referred below). They also received 12 old but valuable seaplanes Heinkel He 114 from Germany (they would have to wait another year to receive 12 Dornier Do 24 modern seaplanes). Thanks to the Bär Program, 10 Stug III and 20 Pz IV also arrived in Spain. Although in general it can be considered that the quantity of war armament supplied by Germany to Spain was very small, taking into account the war situation in Europe and Germany's great need for tanks and aircraft, Germany can be considered as having made an important effort to sell that war material to Spain (the Spanish participation in the Eastern Front with the Blue Division and the Expeditionary Squadrons are sure to have been of great importance at the moment of taking Germany such determination). Later in the text, we will discuss more details of the aircraft shipment by Germany to Spain and the circumstances in which those shipments occurred.

On September 24, 1943, due to the Allies pressure, the Spanish Government was forced to withdraw from the Eastern Front the Blue Division (its last action of war was to repel a Soviet attack on October 5, 1943), but still leaving a small contingent of about 2269 men, in the denominated Blue Legion (Legión Azul), with the purpose of avoiding problems (on the part of the Germans) in the Division repatriation. The latter began to take shape on October 20, 1943, being officially constituted on November 17, as a Regiment under the command of Colonel Antonio García Navarro. The repatriation of the members of the Blue Division was done in stages, being completed before the end of December 1943. The same situation had the members of the Blue Squadron, although this story will be detailed later.

The Allied pressure continued taking advantage of any situation to force Spain to stop supporting Germany (despite the neutrality). The numerous incidents that took place in the Strait of Gibraltar and the Canary Islands areas motivated the USA to request the United Kingdom several diplomatic protests. Obviously, Allied pressure forced Spain to definitively cut off the aid they were providing to Germany. On February 20, 1944, the Führer and Francisco Franco agreed to the repatriation of the Blue Legion. The repatriation order will arrive at the Legionary Command HQ on March 3. On February the 6th at 11.34 am, in the town of Lechts, Colonel García Navarro made his last speech to the legionaries:

"... The news are sad and impressive: Spain, in agreement with the German Government, goes through the painful trance, maybe even tragic, of accessing our repatriation."

"... Come back proud of having done your duty...! Proud because Spain demanded it and because it was done without hesitation".

On the 21st, the last weapons and part of the uniforms were delivered to the Germans, the Legión Azul being considered dissolved the next day, although it would still take about two weeks to deliver their German uniforms in Wilmehoff, to receive the Spaniards themselves. The stipulated retirement of the Blue Legion was carried out in March (the first repatriates arrived in Irún) and April of 1944.

After the withdrawal and dissolution of the Blue Legion (March 1944), the Spanish fighting alongside the Axis was illegal, which did not stop some volunteers to refuse to return to Spain and other Spaniards to cross the border into France towards the Reich. Many of them ended up integrated after many avatars in Units belonging to the Waffen SS (such as the "Wallonien" or the "Norland"), others were assigned to the 3rd Mountain Division or the 357th Infantry Division. Spaniards also fought against the partisan guerrilla in Yugoslavia (August 1944) forming part of the 3rd Regiment 2nd Battalion 8th Company of the Brandenburg Division, which at that time was fighting against the partisan guerrilla in Italy. More information about this unknown part of the Spanish intervention in the WW2 can be found in my book "The Spanish in the SS and Wehrmacht 1944-45. The Ezquerra Unit in the Battle of Berlin".

Although the relations between Spain and Germany were changing during the WW2, in 1944 the German side was still more appreciated in Spain still than the Allies. In fact, although the sales of tungsten to the German Reich had been reduced, (according to Caballero) the Spanish aviation tried to interchange tungsten by aeronautical fuel; but Francisco Franco prevented that commercial pact.

CHAPTER II

Spanish Aviation Reorganization
After The Spanish Civil War

After the bloody Spanish Civil War that took place between 1936 and 1939, Spain had been exhausted and destroyed after declaring the end of the war on April 1. But due to the war years, it had accumulated a large amount of very heterogeneous war material. Regarding the Air Force (known as National Aviation during the Civil War years), we can assure that according to the report sent on February 9, 1940 by the Spanish Air Force general director, it had 1148 aircraft of 95 different models that turned the Spanish Air Force (by number of airplanes) into one of the most numerous in Europe after Germany, Great Britain, France or Italy. The aircraft heterogeneity and the lack of resources led to a high accident rate reaching 105 crew members in the period 1939-1945. At that time, there were more planes than pilots.

The Generalissimo Francisco Franco (head of the Spanish State) approved a new Air Force regional organization (it should have entered into force on July 15, 1939). Thus the Spanish national territory was divided into five Regions (numbered from 1 to 5, and called Central, Strait, Levante, Cantabrian and Pyrenean) and the Atlantic Air Force (which included the Canary Islands, Juby Cape, Ifni and Río de Oro), Balearic Air Forces and Moroccan Air Forces.

We have used the excellent work of González Serrano as the main source of information as well as various works by Arráez Cerda and the Historical Service of the Air Force and the Ministry of Defense on the study of the Air Force during the WW2 years.

The distribution of the airplanes of the EdA will be explained later in detail according to the plane model, although we advance in a global way the aforementioned distribution:

1ª Región Aérea (Air Region)	21 Regimiento (Regiment)	Grupos (Groups) 21 and 22	CR.32
	31 Regimiento	Grupos 31 and 32	He 51
	Regimiento Mixto (Mixed Regiment) nº 1	Grupo 11	Br.20

2ª Región Aérea	11 Regimiento	Grupos 12 and 13	S.79
	12 Regimiento	Grupos 14 and 15	S.79
	22 Regimiento	Mando (HQ) and Grupo 23	CR.32
	---	61 Escuadrilla (Squadron)	Hs 123
3ª Región Aérea	13 Regimiento	Grupos 16 and 17	SB-2
	32 Regimiento	Grupos 33 and 34	I-15
	---	Grupo 24 from 23 Regimiento	I-15bis
4ª Región Aérea	14 Regimiento	Grupos 18 and 19	He 111
	15 Regimiento	Grupos 110 and 111	He 111
	23 Regimiento	Mando and Grupo 25	Bf 109
	---	44 Grupo del Regimiento Mixto nº1 (44 Group from 1st Mixed Regiment)	Do 17
5ª Región Aérea	16 Regimiento	Grupos 112 and 113	S.81
	---	Grupo 26 from 22 Regimiento	CR.32
Fuerzas Aéreas del Protecto-rado de Marruecos (Moroccan Protectorate Air Forces)	Regimiento Mixto nº 2	Grupos 27 and 43	G.50 , He 112, Po0likarpov R-Z
	---	51 Escuadrilla	Dornier Wal
	---	41 Patrulla	Hs 126
Fuerzas Aéreas de Baleares (Balearic Air Forces)	Regimiento Mixto nº 3	Grupos 28 and 51	I-16, He 59, He 60, Cant Z.506, Cant Z.501
Fuerzas Aéreas del Atlántico (Atlantic Air Forces)	---	11 Escuadrilla	Ju 52 Fokker F-XII

As of October 17, 1940, the Cantabrian Region was renamed Atlantic, while the three previous Air Forces became the Morocco Air Zones, West Africa, the Balearic Islands and the Canary Islands. As for the area of the Canary Islands and the nearby Sidi Ifni in the so-called ZACAO (Canary Islands and Africa Air Area), the EdA would later have the Mixed Regiment No.4 equipped with 24 Fiat CR.32, 5 Ju-52 and 2 Dornier Wall.

So the Mixed Regiment nº3 was based in Son San Juan. This unit grouped the 28th Fighter Group and 113 Group since January 1940, all the Balearic aviation belonged to the same units, the Bombing Group Regiment and the Seaplanes Mixed Group. The Seaplane Group had its base in Pollensa and was composed of: the 52 Squadron (with 2 Heinkel 59 and 2 Heinkel He 60, and 3 Arado Ar 95 belonging to the 51 Patrol) and the 53 Squadron (with 2 Cant Z.501 and 2 Cant Z.506B). Throughout 1940 due to events in Europe a dozen Heinkel He-111 bombers were deployed in Son San Juan from Logroño.

But we have to start from the beginning, so on August 8, 1939, the Air Ministry was created, with General Juan Yagüe, a Legion veteran and Germanophile, elected as minister (this election was surprising, since the initial candidate was General Kindelán who had directed the National Aviation during the Civil War, which created some discomfort among the Spanish pilots to feel discriminated). On October 7, 1939 by State´s Headquarters law, the Air Force (EdA) was born. Its assignments

On October 23, 1940 Adolf Hitler and Francisco Franco met in the French town of Hendaye with the intention of Spain joining Germany in the war although the Spanish demands prevented the pact. [Public Domain]

The Spanish ambassador in Berlin, José Finat, together with German and Spanish officers, on the occasion of the dispatch of the 1st Blue Squadron to Russia. To the left of the ambassador is the commander of the 1st Blue Squadron Ángel Salas Larrazabal. July 1941. [Public domain]

Spanish Air Force Insignia, with the colors of the Spanish flag: a circle with the three colors of the Spanish national flag: red in the outside ring - yellow in the middle ring - red in the inner disc. [Free from Public Domain by DV Wiebe]

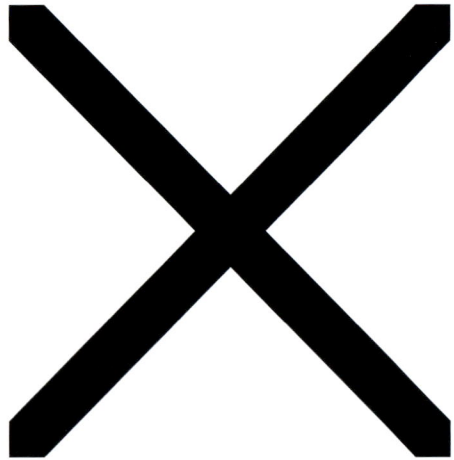

Badge used by the Spanish Air Force planes in the tail. Over a white background it was painted a black Burgundy or St. Jacques Cross. This badge is used nowadays. [Free from Public Domain by Kizar]

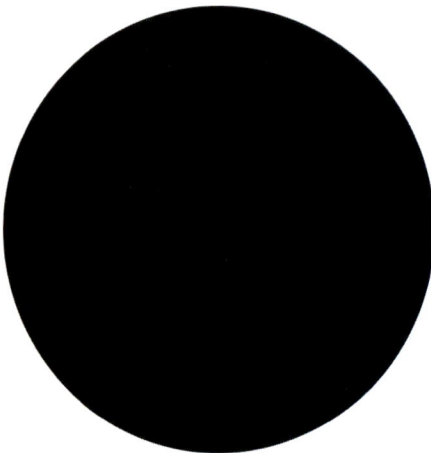

Badge used by the Spanish Nationalist Air Force during SCW and then in the postwar. We can see this black circle in the fuselage of Spanish fighters during WW2.

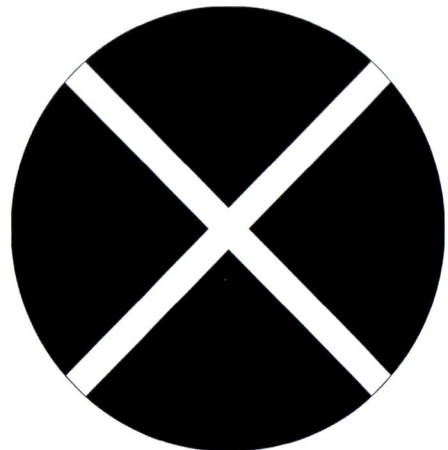

This Badge, a diagonal cross in white on a black background was used during SCW for the Nationalist Air Force in the upper wings. Shortly after the SCW, it was replaced by the three colors insign.

Badge of the Joaquín García Morato Fighter Group with a 2 in roman (II). This was the 1st Blue Squadron ensign. This badge was a white circle with three birds in the center (a hawk, a bustard and a blackbird) and the phrase "Vista, suerte, y al toro" that means "Sight, luck and to the bull".

The Falange badge with the Yoke and the Arrows in white on a black circle background. This badge was used by Spanish Nationalist Air Force during SCW and then in the postwar. This badge without the black circle was used in the Bf 109 of the 2nd Blue Squadron in the fuselage.

Uniform of an Blue Squadron officer. The uniform used by the Spaniards was the same one used by the Germans but with an emblem on the right arm with red-yellow-red colors and the word Spain on top. [Free from Public Domain by Garrapata]

On August 8, 1939, the Spanish Air Ministry was created, and General Juan Yagüe, a veteran of the Legión and Germanophile, was elected as Minister. It was he who made the newly created Air Force try to look structurally like the Luftwaffe. [Public Domain]

Polikapov I-16 "Rat" 1-w-41 in flight. The Polikarpov I-16 "Rat" was destined to the Son San Juan airbase to ensure the protection of the Baleares Islands, but they did not last long, being replaced by the Fiat CR.32. [Courtesy of Juan Arráez Cerdá]

Messerschmitt Bf 109 E-3 in San Javier airbase. These aircraft were the most powerful fighters of the EdA so they were intended to protect the border with France.
[Courtesy of Juan Arráez Cerdá]

Miguel Entrena in the cockpit of his He 112B. [Courtesy of Juan Arráez Cerdá]

Fiat CR.32 in Gando/Las Palmas airbase in charge of defending the Canary Islands. The Gando airfield was an expeditionary group of CR.32s sent by boat (from the Getafe Air Base) in order to protect the Canary Islands. [Courtesy of Juan Arráez Cerdá]

The meteorological Heinkel He 111J 25-111, in Barajas. [Courtesy of Juan Arráez Cerdá]

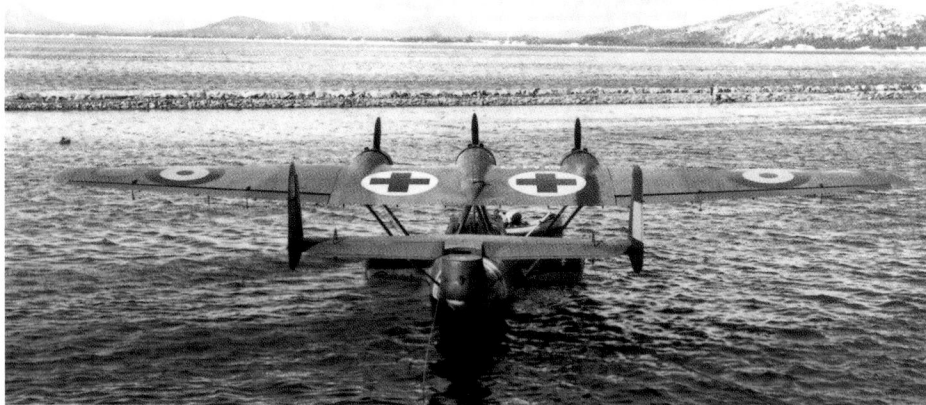
Dornier Do 24T.3 acquired in Germany for the Maritime rescue in the Western Mediterranean.
[Courtesy of Juan Arráez Cerdá]

Focke Wulf FW 200 "Condor" F8 + HA interned in Seville.
[Courtesy of Juan Arráez Cerdá]

Several Spanish pilots belonging to the 1st Blue Squadron over one of their Bf 109 Es. From left to right: Lieutenants O'Connors, Carracido, Zorita and Bartolomé. [Courtesy of Juan Arráez Cerdá]

Consolidated Catalina OA-10 of the U.S. Army Air Force, interned in Spanish Northern Morocco. At the end of the WW2 was acquired and entered into service with the Spanish Air Force. [Courtesy of Juan Arráez Cerdá]

Messerschmitt Bf 109E.3 in El Prat / Barcelona, located there for the defense of the French border. [Courtesy of Juan Arráez Cerdá]

Italian Romeo Ro.43 interned in Pollensa when the Badoglio coup d´etat. It passed to the Ejército del Aire. [Courtesy of Juan Arráez Cerdá]

A 52 Bombing Regiment Savoia S.79 based in Armilla (Granada) They were sent to Son San Juan (Mallorca) for the surveillance of maritime routes. This plane, the 28-59 was the couple of S.79 shot down by the British near the Baleares Islands, and in this photograph is in Barajas in 1942. [Courtesy of Juan Arráez Cerdá]

Several Heinkel He 45 used as an advanced training plane, we see them at the San Javier airbase (Murcia) at the beginning of the 40s. [Courtesy of Juan Arráez Cerdá]

Captain Aristides Lopez Garcia-Rengel of the 1st Blue Squadron smiling in the cockpit of his Bf 109 E. Shortly thereafter he would disappear in combat. [Courtesy of Juan Arráez Cerdá]

Commander Ángel Salas of the 1st Blue Squadron is greeted by the Oberstleutnant Werner Mölders and between them the Commander José Muñoz Jiménez "El Corto". The three of them were good friends since the times of the SCW. [Courtesy of Juan Arráez Cerdá]

At the Orel airbase we see this Bf 109 F-2 belonging to the 2nd Blue Squadron that has been painted the legend CABO MECANICO ZARO !PRESENTE!, in honor of Tomas Zaro Rubio, who died on July 28, 1942 when he was hit by the propeller of the 109 he was checking. In the fuselage and next to the Balkenkreuz carries the emblem of the Yoke and the Arrows from Falange Española de las JONS (National Syndicalist Offensive Council Spanish Falange). [Courtesy of Juan Arráez Cerdá]

The members of the 2nd Blue Squadron, at the Werneuchen airfield in Berlin, where they trained, wearing the German uniform for the first time. [Courtesy of Juan Arráez Cerdá]

Julio Salvador, the Inspector Commander of the 2nd Blue Squadron, talking about the plane he shot down with his partner Lieutenant Ramón Escudé. [Courtesy of Juan Arráez Cerdá]

On March 6, 1943, Ensign Alfonso Texidor "Retaco" of the 3rd Blue Squadron shot down a LaGG-3 piloted by Captain Mikhail Korpkovo. In the photograph we see the two men; "Retaco" appears on the left side of the Russian, who is escorted by a Gendarme. [Courtesy of Juan Arráez Cerdá]

The two best hunters of the 3rd Blue Squadron, Captain Hevia and Lieutenant Azqueta, along with one of the new Fw 190 that Germans have handed over to the Spaniards. [Courtesy of Juan Arráez Cerdá]

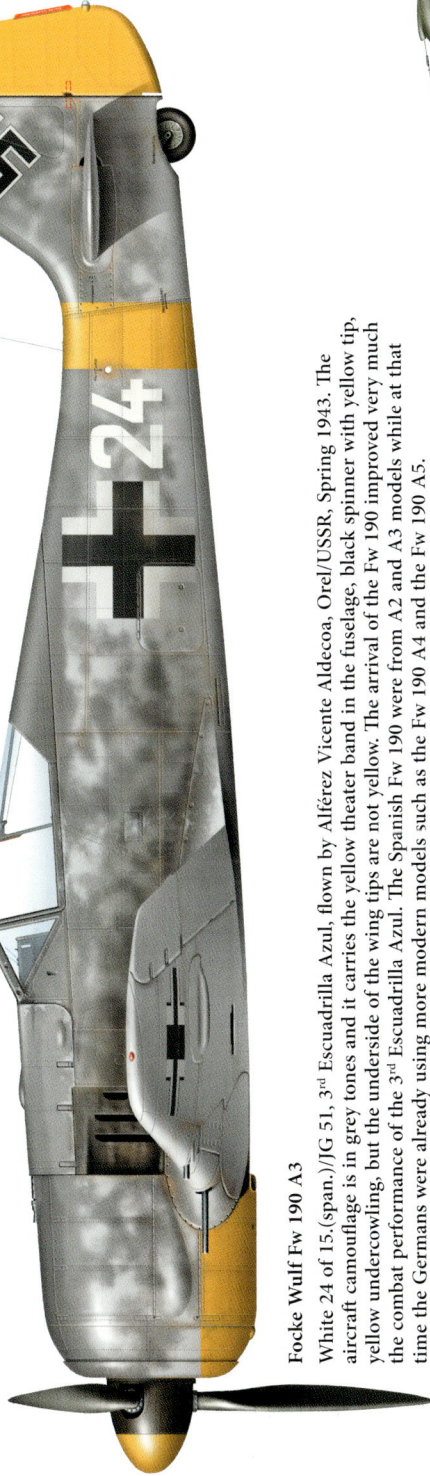

Focke Wulf Fw 190 A3

White 24 of 15.(span.)/JG 51, 3rd Escuadrilla Azul, flown by Alférez Vicente Aldecoa. Orel/USSR, Spring 1943. The aircraft camouflage is in grey tones and it carries the yellow theater band in the fuselage, black spinner with yellow tip, yellow undercowling, but the underside of the wing tips are not yellow. The arrival of the Fw 190 improved very much the combat performance of the 3rd Escuadrilla Azul. The Spanish Fw 190 were from A2 and A3 models while at that time the Germans were already using more modern models such as the Fw 190 A4 and the Fw 190 A5.

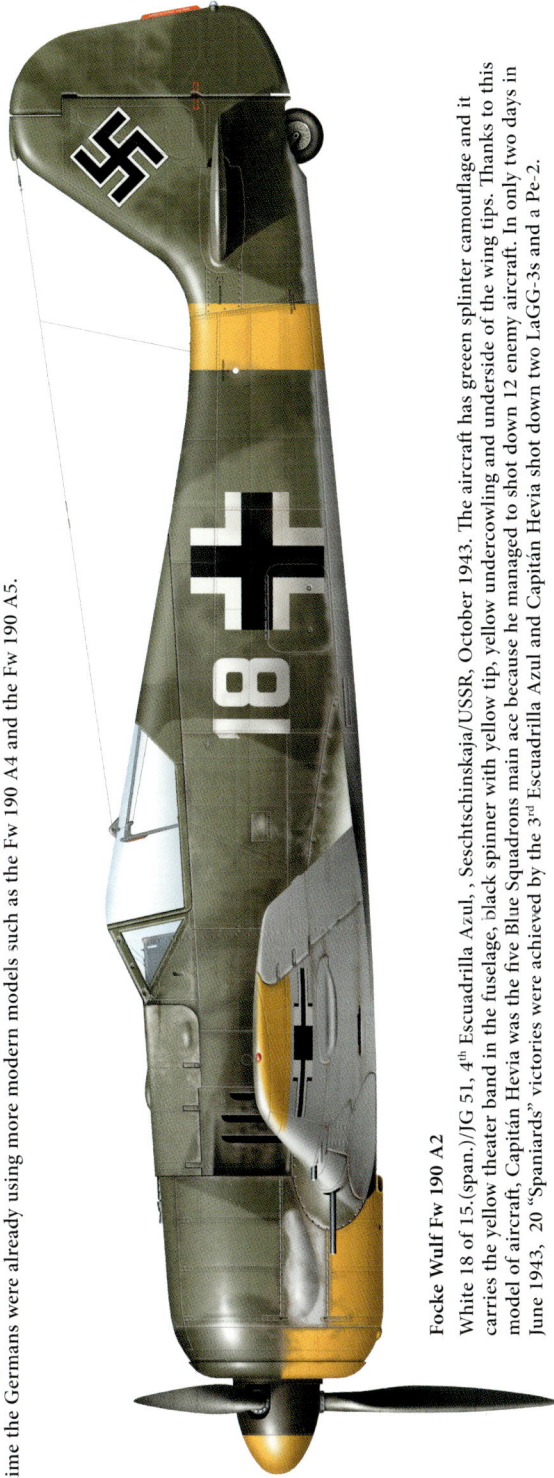

Focke Wulf Fw 190 A2

White 18 of 15.(span.)/JG 51, 4th Escuadrilla Azul, , Seschtschinskaja/USSR, October 1943. The aircraft has green splinter camouflage and it carries the yellow theater band in the fuselage, black spinner with yellow tip, yellow undercowling and underside of the wing tips. Thanks to this model of aircraft, Capitán Hevia was the five Blue Squadrons main ace because he managed to shot down 12 enemy aircraft. In only two days in June 1943, 20 "Spaniards" victories were achieved by the 3rd Escuadrilla Azul and Capitán Hevia shot down two LaGG-3s and a Pe-2.

Painted by Arkadiusz Wróbel

Focke Wulf Fw 190 A2

White 12 of 15.(span.)/JG 51, 4th Escuadrilla Azul, flown by Teniente José Cavanilles Vereterra, Smolensk airfield /USSR, September 1943. The aircraft carries the yellow theater band in the fuselage, yellow undercowling, underside of the wing tips and spinner. José Cavanilles (known as Pepin Cavanilles) achieved four air victories and was shot down and killed in this aircraft during an air combat (approximately 5 German aircraft and 2 Spaniards protected 27 Ju 87s, who were attacked by numerous Soviet aircraft 5 times larger) South-East of the town of Cawydowitschi on 10 January 1944.

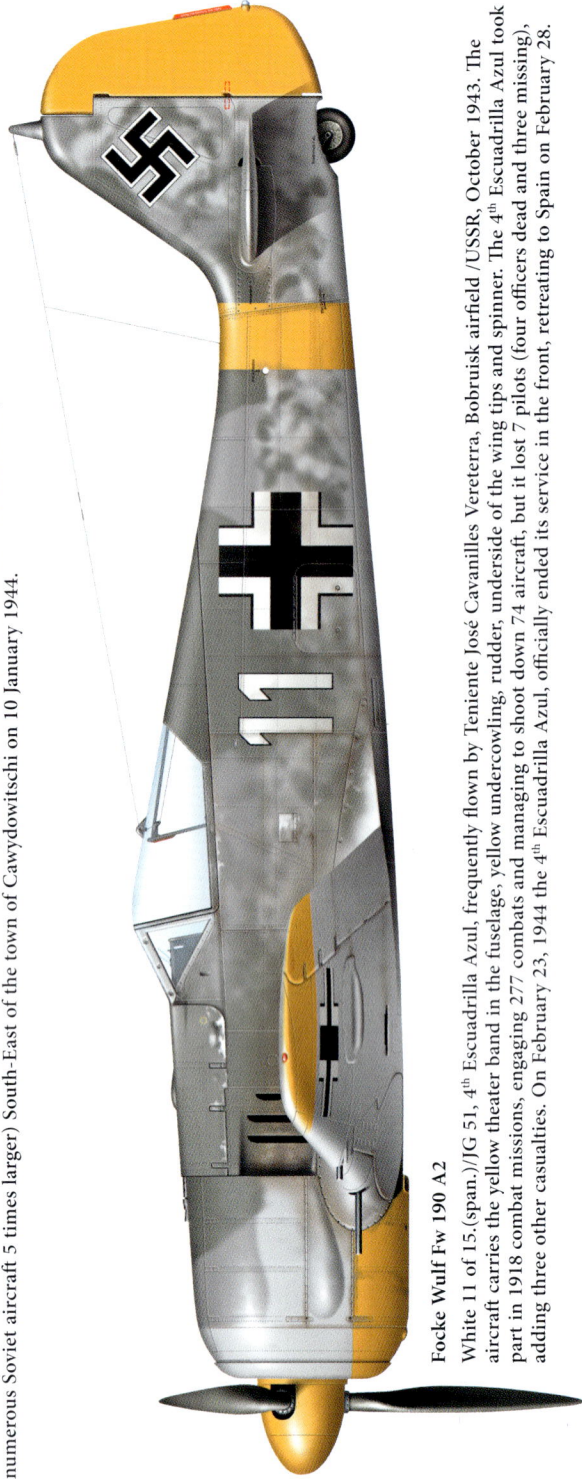

Focke Wulf Fw 190 A2

White 11 of 15.(span.)/JG 51, 4th Escuadrilla Azul, frequently flown by Teniente José Cavanilles Vereterra, Bobruisk airfield /USSR, October 1943. The aircraft carries the yellow theater band in the fuselage, yellow undercowling, rudder, underside of the wing tips and spinner. The 4th Escuadrilla Azul took part in 1918 combat missions, engaging 277 combats and managing to shoot down 74 aircraft, but it lost 7 pilots (four officers dead and three missing), adding three other casualties. On February 23, 1944 the 4th Escuadrilla Azul, officially ended its service in the front, retreating to Spain on February 28.

included "the fundamental one to develop all its offensive power by means of its air units". On November 9, the Aviation Weapon was created, as the main element and axis of the EdA. On December 15, the Aeronautical Engineers Corps was created within the EdA.

Before his appointment, Yagüe had traveled to Germany as part of the Spanish mission that accompanied the return of the Legion Condor. There, he took the opportunity to learn many details of the Luftwaffe structure and organization, which was the example to be followed by military aviation in Spain. During the 10 months that General Yagüe led the ministry (he was ceased in June 1940 and replaced by Juan Vigón who was not an aviator either), he drew the operational and organizational lines to be followed by the EdA, which was none other than the one of the German Luftwaffe. Although many of Yagüe's ideas were finally fulfilled (his plan marked the development of the EdA in the following years after WW2), one of the illusions that was evidently never fulfilled was getting 5,000 aircraft in the EdA in a time of only 5 years since his arrival at the ministry.

Within the new aviation organization, it was established that the air units would be according to their use; Fighter, assault, bombing, dive bombing, seaplanes and reconnaissance. The Air Units that were formed went from smaller to larger size: the Squadron, the Group and the Regiment (Squad).

The first task entrusted to the EdA was to collect and put in flight conditions all the aircraft abandoned by the Republican Army. This task was not at all immediate, since it was necessary to wait until the first half of 1940 when some of the Republican airplanes that had fled to France were recovered.

Obviously the conservation and operation state in which these aircraft were found was very different. For this reason, it was necessary to determine which aircraft would be in the inventory of the EdA and which ones could be put up for sale or in some cases, those that would become scrap.

A final fact that we have to assess is about the EdA pilots. Most of them had fought during the Spanish Civil War. In the three years of the conflict, the pilots were maturing and "professionalizing", so that at the fighting ability skill they were not inferior to the other countries pilots. His German comrades, members of the Legion Condor, were able to fight with them in the skies of Spain and were pleasantly impressed with their tenacity and courage. In this regard, the Aviation officers increased from 1639 in February 1939 to 2093 in January 1945. Regarding non-commissioned officers and troops, a similar situation happened, although in greater numbers than in officers.

A very important fact to take into account is that in the aeronautical sphere, Spain collaborated with the Axis; as shown by the authorizations and facilities that were given to Germans and Italians in Spain. Even German reconnaissance aircraft flew with Spanish badges (we will later discuss about the Meteorological Squadron). In

October 1941, taking advantage of the first successes of the Blue Squadron in Russia, Colonel Roa, new Air Ministry Industry and Equipment General Director began to pressure the Germans to get more help for Spanish military Aviation.

Also in Spain, infrastructures were created to help the Luftwaffe air navigation, as well as certain facilities to navigate through Spanish airspace. With the passing of the years and the next Axis defeat, Spain had to yield to the Allies, limiting the collaboration with the Axis at first and later offering support to the Allies (since 1944, concessions were made regarding the Allied air traffic towards to Central Europe and in February 1945 the agreement with USA for the use of Juby Cape and Villa Cisneros aerodromes was allowed to the Air Transport Command Airplanes).

In the following chapters when we will know about the deployment of EdA fighters, bombers, etc, then we will show the most important locations of each of the aircraft groups, although there were several minor deployment modifications during the WW2 years, which in some cases we will obviate because this text does not have such an exhaustive purpose.

CHAPTER III

The Fighter Groups

Within the text we are going to divide the activities of the Spanish Fighter branch into two sections. A first section will deal with the performance of Spanish fighters protecting Spanish airspace (including the Northern Africa and Western Africa Protectorate territories) to what we will call „National Defense"; being the second section dedicated to the performance of Spanish pilots with German aircraft that formed the Expeditionary Squadrons in Russia to what we will call „The Russian Front: The Blue Squadrons"; which, although they did not belong to the EdA, were obviously officially members of the EdA.

In the section about „National Defense" we will not only write about the planes deployment, but we will also write about the incidents with belligerent countries airplanes, both with Spanish aircraft and with anti-aircraft artillery.

Both in the „National Defense" and in „The Russian Front: the Blue Squadrons", the Spanish pilots flew both the skies of Spain and Russia, demonstrating their value and skill in the flight.

The National Defense

DEPLOYMENT

For this part of the text, we have used several information sources, highlighting the exceptional and superb text by José Luis González Serrano. The Fighter aviation (like the other branches of the EdA) after finishing the SCW, was concentrated in the airfields of Alcalá de Henares (in Madrid) waiting to be deployed following the regulations issued by General Kindelán. Thus, as of June 1939, the fighters began to be sent to different aerodromes belonging to the different Air Regions, being distributed as follows:

- Central Air Region: At the Getafe airbase (near Madrid), most of the Spanish fighters (Escuadra de Caza) were deployed with a command patrol and two CR.32 Groups.

- Strait of Gibraltar Air Region: at the Tablada airbase (near Seville) a CR.32 Group was deployed (with a command patrol and two squadrons).

- Levante Air Region: at the Manises airbase (near Valencia) an I-15bis Group (two squadrons) was deployed.
- Pirineo Air Region: At the Agoncillo airbase (near Logroño) a Bf 109 Group was deployed (with a command patrol and four squadrons).
- Cantabrian Air Region: at the Virgen del Camino airbase in León, a CR.32 Group was deployed (with a command patrol and four squadrons).
- Moroccan Air Forces: at the Nador airbase (although the airbase name was Tauima) was deployed a pursuit group with 2 squadrons (one equipped with Fiat G.50 and another equipped with Heinkel He 112B).
- Balearic Air Force: At the Son San Juan airbase, a Polikarpov I-16 "Rat" Group was deployed (with a command patrol and four squadrons).

As we can see, the Canary Islands had not initially deployed fighter aircraft, due to the "quietness" existing in that geographical area in 1939. Evidently this would change shortly afterwards as we will describe later on what would be called ZACAO or Canary Islands Air and West Africa (the Sidi Ifni) Areas.

Another curious detail, proof of how "young" the EdA was, was that no numbering system was used to name the different units. This changed on September 1, 1939 when "the enumeration of squadrons, groups, independent squads and independent patrols will be done before the corresponding number, the indicative of the aircraft type, this being 1 for Bombing, 2 for Fighter, 3 for Assault, 4 for Reconnaissance, 5 for Seaplanes and 6 for Dive Bombers" and "the numbering of the Squadrons within their Groups will be 1st, 2nd, 3rd, etc ". Shortly thereafter, on November 9, the Squad was replaced by the Regiment (formed by several Groups that could have different types planes, then the basic tactical unit was the Squadron).

In January 1940 the distribution of the Spanish fighters was as follows (based in José Luis González Serrano work):

Regiment	Group	Base	Aircraft	Number
21	21	Getafe	CR.32	33
21	22	Getafe	CR.32	30
	23	Tablada	CR.32	26
	24	Manises	I-15bis	20
	25	Agoncillo	Bf 109	41
	26	León	CR.32	35
	27	Nador	G.50 , He 112	20
	28	Son San Juan	I-16	11
				216

As it is reasonable to think, the total number of Spanish fighters was 126, but the operative fighters number was lower (161).

With the world conflict, changes began to be made in the initial fighter's deployment. For example in January 1940, Group 26 moved from León to Mallorca (Son

San Juan). Subsequently more transfers occurred, so to simplify and based on the text of José Luis González Serrano, we will indicate the deployment to January 1941:

Regiment	Group	Base	Aircraft	Number
21	21	Getafe	CR.32	54
21	22	Gando (Gran Canaria)	CR.32	25
22	23	Tablada	CR.32	29
23	24	Manises	I-15bis	18
23	25	El Prat (Barcelona)	Bf 109	36
22	26	Son San Juan	CR.32	22
Mixto 2	27	Nador	G.50 , He 112	21
Mixto 3	28	Son San Juan	I-16	1
				206 (131 ready to fly)

In January 1942 the deployment was as follows (based in José Luis González Serrano work):

Regiment	Group	Base	Aircraft	Number
21	21	Getafe	CR.32	60
21	22	Gando (Gran Canaria) then to Getafe	CR.32	-
22	23	Tablada	CR.32	13
23	24	Reus (Tarragona)	I-15bis	18
23	25	Reus (Tarragona)	Bf 109	30
22	26	Tablada	I-16	5
Mixto 2	27	Nador	G.50 , He 112	22
Mixto 3	28	Son San Juan	CR.32	23
Mixto 4	29	Gando (Gran Canaria)	CR.32	6
				177 (76 ready to fly)

And the deployment during 1944 until mid-1945 was as follows (based in José Luis González Serrano work):

Regiment	Group	Base	Aircraft	Number
21	21	Getafe	CR.32	30-53
21	22	Getafe	CR.32	12-21
22	23	Tablada	CR.32	22-27
23	24	Reus (Tarragona)	I-15bis	11-12
23	25	Reus (Tarragona)	Bf 109	10-19
22	26	Tablada	I-16	12-21
Mixto 2	27	Nador	G.50 , He 112	15-16
Mixto 3	28	Son San Juan	CR.32	23-27
Mixto 4	29	Gando (Gran Canaria)	CR.32	23-28
				175-214

As we can see the aircraft types that were available in 1939 were the same as in 1945, so they were even more obsolete and their conservation status was decreasing and were in poor condition due to the difficulty of being able to make adequate maintenance. When jet planes were already flying in the skies of Europe, the biplanes I-15bis and Cr.32 were still flying in Spain.

Air Incidents With Allied Aircraft

The privileged Spain´s geographical situation as the Mediterranean "gate" and the Cantabrian Sea, African Atlantic coast and the western Mediterranean made Spain a country in a very strategic location for both bands. This situation motivated that even if Spain remained neutral, its air space was overflowed by different nations involved in the war military aircraft. These belligerent countries aircraft flights were in some cases accidental, but in many other cases they were completely deliberate or even necessary to save the lives of the aircraft crew. In general, the conflicts derived from the Spanish airspace violation were almost exclusively with Allies aircraft, due to the different Spaniards attitude with the Axis aircraft (although there were still some incidents with the Vichy France aircraft). The Spanish airspace violations by the Allies and Germany were frequent, leading to air strikes that ended in some occasions with the shot down of Spanish aircraft and in fewer cases with the shot down of Allied aircraft. There were also Spanish planes shot down when they were "confused" with the enemy.

In this chapter we will also report some incidents with Allied airplanes in which the Spanish antiaircraft artillery tried to defend the Spanish airspace.

Shot Down Spanish Aircraft

On December 18, 1939, the Ju 52 M-CABA belonging to the Iberia Spanish airline, which was traveling through Seville-Tetouan (in the North Africa Spanish Protectorate), was shot down over Algeciras by a British destroyer (other sources suggest that it was a lightning the cause). The legendary Ju 52/3m transport aircraft used by Spain was the same as those used by the Germans, so it was not complicated to confuse the silhouette of this Spanish aircraft with a German one. In spite of this, the British with this type of actions tried to emphasize their dominion of the area near the Gibraltar Strait. In this case, a short time later, a British plane was shot down by the Spanish anti-aircraft artillery on Tarifa.

On November 8, 1940, a new unfortunate clash between a Spanish aircraft and some RAF fighters took place near the Balearic Islands. It was a Spanish Savoia S.79 bomber belonging to Bomber Regiment 12, exactly the same kind of plane as those used by the Italian aviation (Regia Aeronautica) on its flights over the Mediterranean Sea waters, so there was a confusion again that resulted lethal since the 5 crew members died. Two S.79 aircraft took off at 14.00 p.m. from Son San Juan aerodrome heading south. At 3:00 pm the plane numbered 28-59 lost sight of its companion (numbered 28-62), after looking for it and not finding it, the pilot finally flew towards the Son San Juan airbase where the bomber landed at 17.35 pm (during the return flight) glimpsed in the distance what appeared to be a large naval convoy, while simultaneously the Son San Juan control tower heard gunfire sound in an SOS message from 28-62). The cause of the loss of the Spanish plane was the S.79 proximity to the Royal Navy's "H" Force, which carried out attacks against southern Sardinia (as ruse attacks for "Operation Judgment" intended to carry out the attack on Taranto). The Spanish plane followed about 6 minutes the "H" Force, which allowed the British to consider it as a hostile plane. A Fairey Fulmar belonging to 808 Naval Air Squadron left to search for the S.79 and after locating it, made two attacks that finally brought down the Spanish plane. After having lost contact with the bomber, they set out on their search from their base in Son San Juan (Mallorca) as well as from the Pollensa seaplane base, but they only found the aircraft wrecks floating in the water. This Royal Navy act shooting down a neutral plane motivated the Spanish Government protests, but the British simply justified themselves by saying that they believed it was an Italian plane and that it was going to attack the fleet. There was always the question of whether they really knew that it was a Spanish plane.

Incidents With Allied Aircraft

Most of the incidents with allied aircraft took place in two geographical areas: the Gibraltar Strait (including the southern Iberian Peninsula and the North Africa Spanish Protectorate) and the Canary Islands. Since the beginning of WW2, British aircraft based in Gibraltar (in Spanish mainland) already had a lot of clashes with their neutral Spanish neighbors (RAF Supermarine Spitfires and Hurricanes caused many problems to Spaniards, although without having to regret the shot down of any plane). Although the Allies knew the prohibition of flying over the airspace of a neutral country, the Allied pilots also knew that flying over Spanish territory allowed them to reduce the distances to fly (using Spanish airspace as a shortcut). There were many occasions in which Allied aircraft were interned in Spanish airspace and intercepted by Spanish fighters (Fiat G.50 and especially by the Heinkel He 112). Fortunately, the orders of the Spanish pilots were to warn the belligerent pilots who were flying over neutral territory and who had to abandon it, always with orders not to open fire.

But all these clashes in the southern Spain skies and the air traffic increase in the Spanish "shortcut" in the North Africa territories were increased from November 1942 with the beginning of "Operation Torch", the Allied landing in the area of

French Morocco and in Algeria to neutralize the French colonies loyal to Vichy France. Once the positions in northwest Africa were taken, the next objective was to expel the Italian-German forces that fought against the Allied forces in Tunisia and Libya.

The strain in the Spanish Protectorate area motivated the USA President to send a personal letter to the Spanish Leader, General Franco, in which he guaranteed that the Allies military operations in North Africa were not directed in any way against the overseas Spanish territories. The Spanish authorities objected incessantly to the Anglo-American command, who gave little importance to the complaints. Despite American good intentions, Franco was aware of how difficult it would be if there were no incidents with the Allies, so more units of the Army were deployed and the presence of the EdA was reinforced in the area with more aircraft to protect the Canary Islands and the Spanish possessions in North Africa airspace. In fact, the Heinkel He 112, which were the best Spanish fighters at that time, were all deployed at the base of Nador (Melilla).

In addition as another defense measure against possible Spanish airspace invasions, the Larache, Ceuta, Tangier, Tetouan, Axdir and Alhucemas military airfields (all belonging to North Africa Spanish territories), were put on high alert . A defense and passive warning system was created, formed by a warning and listening network located along the Spanish coast that used telegraphic and radio communications to raise the alarm in case of locating intruders in the Spanish country. Once the warning was given, the nearest aerodrome was informed (basically the one in Nador, which was the one that received the most incursions from belligerent planes) where a plane prepared for an immediate emergency take-off should always be prepared, just as it happened in other air forces in WW2 and still happens today.

Simultaneously with "Operation Torch", on November 8, 1942, the Spanish fighters based in Nador intercepted near Melilla a C-47 Skytrains flight formation loaded with paratroopers without fighter escort in Estutel. Following the orders received, the Spanish pilots escorted the Allied transport planes out of the Spanish national airspace.

On March 3, 1943 a formation of P-38 allied fighter-bombers violated Spanish sovereignty again by flying over Spanish territory in North Africa from Algeria. The information of the appearance of the Allied airplanes was sent urgently to the Nador airbase where the fighters belonging to the 27th Fighter Group immediately received the order to take off to intercept them. It was (as it could be known later) a flight with 11 American P-38 Lightning belonging to the 12th Air Corps 14th Fighter Group (joint Anglo-American unit belonging to the North West African Allied Air Force) based on Youk-les -Bains (Algeria). The fighter-bombers flew in two flights with five and six aircraft at different heights.

As we know, the base of Nador had two types of fighters: the Heinkel He 112 B (1st Squadron) and the Fiat G-50 (2nd Squadron). Due to the danger that the American fighter-bombers represented, it was decided to choose the fastest and most powerful He 112 B to intercept them. The pilot who was ready for the immediate emergency takeoff was Lieutenant Miguel Entrena Klett. After receiving the information of the American planes, he took off with his He 112 B immediately and headed to meet the P-38.

Lieutenant Entrena Klett ascended his plane to 3,500 m altitude, locating the P-38 formation. After evaluating the situation, he decided to ascend to 4000 meters and position his He 112 B between the sun and the American planes. They approached the P-38 formation that was flying in formation at higher altitude and due to the refusal to leave the Spanish airspace, they launched a fast attack against the formation last P-38 (a P-38 F-1).

In evident numerical inferiority and boasting of great value, Lieutenant Entrena Klett fired his two 20 mm guns and damaged one of the P-38 engines, which began to burn and smoke. Although Entrena also fired its machine guns, no projectiles came out of them (later, when the He 112 B landed, Entrena checked that the gunsmiths had forgotten to load the machine guns). The damaged P-38 had to leave the flight formation and threw the fuel drop tank (these would later be recovered in Spanish territory by Spanish soldiers who could of 20 mm projectiles check holes in these drop tanks).

The Spanish pilot was placed near the damaged P-38 and forced him to bail out, although the American pilot preferred to remain in flight to avoid falling into Spanish territory and avoid being interned in Spain. Thus he managed to fly with his plane to the Spanish-French border between Morocco and Algeria avoiding a capture by the Spaniards. The American pilot made a forced landing with only one wheel on the Mulluya River banks (right on the border between the French territory controlled by the Allies and Spanish territory), causing serious damage to the plane landing. The next day US troops recovered the plane wreckage.

The Americans answer did not take long, since that same day 21 North American fighters in several formations (flying in 7 "Vees") challenged the Spaniards flying low over the Nador aerodrome. Evidently the Spaniards did not receive orders to go out in defense of the aerodrome to avoid air clashes against the powerful American airplanes.

Reckoning in depth this American aircraft shot down by the Spanish fighter despite its neutrality, we have to think that the consequences of this incident could have been very serious for Spain. The P-38 shot down belonging to the 14th Fighter Group and the subsequent American retaliation over Nador could have meant the entry of Spain into WW2. Fortunately for Spain, an urgent diplomatic negotiation was initiated in which the incident was justified as an excess of zeal of the Spanish pilot to protect neutrality and Spanish airspace; and that finally did not give rise to the start of hostilities against Spain by the Allies. Thanks to the efforts of the Spanish Government, the tension in North Africa was reduced. To finally close the incident, one month after the P-38 shot down, Lieutenant Entrena became part of the Complement Scale.

From that moment on, the order had to be given to the Spanish pilots, who in the case of intercepting planes without authorization to fly over Spanish territory in North Africa, would only be authorized to shoot in the case of being attacked. Evidently this fact was used by the Allies to continue making fun of the Spaniards by illegally crossing Spanish air space whenever they wanted.

Just a few days after the American P-38 F-1 shot down, another P-38 plane landed in Melilla after the pilot got lost. The plane was captured by the Spaniards but only to be transferred to the Nador airfield (the pilot was the 27th Fighter Group boss, Captain Miguel Guerrero García).

But the relative tranquility would end shortly afterwards, because between October 26 and November 1, 1943 several serious incidents occurred with mainly American aircraft in the Canary Islands. These Allied airplanes flights were mainly in maritime reconnaissance tasks, reason why Catalina or Ventura planes made flights on Spanish territorial waters. This geographical area, being less important than the one in North Africa, did not have adequate Fighter aircraft to carry out interceptions of the most modern and fast American planes. In particular they were the obsolete 29th Fighter Group Fiat CR.32s based in Gando (Tenerife) those with their Breda-Safat machine guns trying to defend the Spanish Canary Islands sovereignty. Along with them, the antiaircraft artillery tried in turn to prevent the transit of belligerent aircraft over Canary territory (although these were deployed only in some strategic areas).

There were many clashes in which the Spanish planes went out to meet the Americans. Having no other way to communicate with the planes entering Spanish airspace, they fired warning bursts that were sometimes interpreted as attacks by Allied planes, which responded to the threatening enemy fire by firing.

On October 26, 1943 a Fiat CR.32 "Chirri" (according to other sources on October 28) attacked a PBY-5A Catalina of the VP-73 about 9 kilometers east of Melenara (according to Spanish sources, quite possibly the plane American was just 2 kilometers from Gando). The attack consisted of two warning firing bursts that the "Chirri" made to the seaplane. The problem was that the bullets hit the plane 10 times and a crew member got injured. The Catalina fled and returned to his base without responding to the Spanish plane fire. As a curiosity, the Americans thought in this case as in others carried out by the "Chirri" that these had been carried out by Cr.42, which were never in service in the EdA.

Possibly on October 28, 1943, there were two Lockheed PV-1 Ventura of the VP-127 (another source refers to the VP-73 of the US Navy) that "being threatened" by the presence of a "Chirri" from the airfield of Gando, shot the Fiat CR.32 . The Spanish plane received several impacts on its fuselage, but the pilot did not receive any damage. In spite of its lower speed and armament, the Spanish pilot tried to respond but could not do it because their Breda-Safat machine guns jammed. After that, the two American Venturas tried to provoke the Spaniards by flying over the city of Las Palmas for 20 minutes without receiving any damage from the anti-aircraft batteries that shot the Americans.

On November 1, 1943 (October 29 according to other sources), another serious incident occurred between a "Chirri" from Gando and a PBY-5A Catalina. About 12 kilometers east (according to other sources, the distance was not more than 3 kilometers) of Melenara, Lieutenant Pascual Macía attacked an American Catalina VP-73 (a British Catalina from the base of Gibraltar according to other sources). The Catalina fired shots at the Spanish plane when approaching, reason why the pilot of the Cr.32 when making the warning shots caused 40 impacts in the first attack, injuring three of its crew and causing serious damage to the plane (possibly the nerves in both pilots confused the intentions of the other one). Later, the seaplane crew answered to the Spanish plane fire without causing damage, while the Spanish pilot continued to make passes to force them to retire. The Catalina had to flee in very bad conditions. At last the Catalina had to make an emergency landing on the Agadir beach (Morocco).

Based on these incidents that once again created an emergency situation in Spanish diplomacy, it was agreed with the Allies that reconnaissance aircraft could not get closer than five kilometers from the coast. This stopped the incidents with the Canary Islands "Chirris". Also the Spanish airplanes chronic lack of fuel motivated that the venerable "Chirris" practically stopped to fly starting from March of 1944. The war was already decided and the Spanish Government began to make approaches to the Allies, like the pact with the USA for allowing the use of some Spanish aerodromes to American airplanes (such as the aerodromes of Madrid or the one in Cabo Juby or Juby Cape).

Incidents With The Anti-Air Artillery

Apart from war aviation, the other weapon that Spain could use to defend its territory from the planes of the belligerent countries was anti-aircraft artillery. Even before the WW2 began, there were already orders in Spain to shoot at British planes flying over Spanish territory. Already in 1940, with the war started, the order was given for the fighters to intervene against planes not authorized to fly over Spanish territory.

The fact that Spain was neutral in WW2 did not prevent high tension situations in Spanish airspace due to the two opposing bands. Again, the areas with the greatest possibility of conflicts with unauthorized aircraft were the Gibraltar Strait and the Canary Islands (in fact the Spanish collaborationism with the Axis from the first WW2 years generated pressure from the Allies that threatened directly to the Canary Islands).

The situation of Gibraltar with its important British operations base motivated numerous incidents in which in some occasions the British airplanes had to be warned, with the firings of the Spanish artillery. In the south of Spain and African Spanish Protectorate territory, due to the proximity of the French bases in Algeria and Morocco, there were also multiple incidents (mainly by air space invasions) to which anti-aircraft artillery answered sometimes. Fortunately, these clashes usually ended without any damage on either side.

In the Canary Islands and the Spanish Western Africa provinces, the first warning shots of the antiaircraft artillery date from January of 1943 in Cabo Juby and later in the Canary Islands from April of 1943. An example was the antiaircraft artillery existing in the Gran Canaria island, which was formed by 8 Flak-14 75mm guns (of German origin) and 3 76,2/55 model 31 guns (of Soviet origin), both coming from the SCW; in addition there were some 24 20mm machine guns and about 10 7.92mm machine guns. All the artillery was concentrated in Las Palmas (the capital of the island), Puerto de la Luz and the Gando air base.

Due to the increase of cases in which the Allied planes bothered to the Spanish antiaircraft defenses, it was ordered to identify the intruder plane (to later being able to make the diplomatic claim due to the transgressive of the international regulations in this matter) and in the event that it persisted in its defiant attitude on Spanish territory two shots would be made in front of and to the left of the intruder plane. Only in the case of not leaving the Spanish airspace, then the aggressor plane would be shot.

The Canary Islands and its nearby waters became, since March 1941, a clandestine supply zone for German submarines (between March and July 1941, 6 U-Bootes in the Puerto de la Luz). Apparently the Germans had two bases that served as support in the Canary Islands, a secondary in the Santa Cruz de Tenerife harbor and another principal one in Puerto de la Luz (in Gran Canaria); the latter being the preferred one and the one that was normally used for the submarines replenishment.

The Allies quickly had reports indicating the presence of the "Grey Wolves" in the Canary Islands, so they began to make many observation flights over the Spanish islands. Although the pressure of the Allies caused that Spain officially did not allow the supply of submarines since July 1941, the surveillance of the Canary Islands did not diminish until the last year of WW2. From November 13, 1942, the squadrons VP-92 (VP-63?) and VP-73 arrived in Casablanca and Port Lyautey and operated on the Atlantic waters (as well as the USAAF 480th Group 2 squadrons since March 1943). The reason was the distrust on the part of the Allies that Spain did not help the Germans, reason why they used their marine reconnaissance airplanes to verify the German maritime presence in those waters of the Atlantic. In fact the suspicions of the Allies were confirmed when the sinking of the type IXC/40 U-167 oceanic submarine by a Hudson Mk.III belonging to 233th Squadron of the RAF in the Burras bay (in Gran Canaria) took place in April 1943 and U-135 between Fuerteventura and Cabo Juby in July 1943.

After these incidents, the Allied reconnaissance missions became much more frequent and were violated on more than one occasion the Spanish airspace (which reached up to 5 kilometers from the coast). The increasing number of clashes between Spaniards and Allies finally forced Spain (specifically Minister Francisco Gómez Jordana as head of Spanish diplomacy) to withdraw the order to shoot at airplanes that violated the airspace (although it was not completely fulfilled, since it allowed to shoot against the planes that did not pay attention to the warning and fly over Spanish territory). But the incidents would repeat themselves in the first months of 1944, especially in the area of the Tenerife island.

The following are examples of the Spanish antiaircraft artillery use. There were 136 shots and in 1944 a total of 54 shots by the antiaircraft artillery only from the Gran Canaria island in 1943 (during the period between 1943 and the first quarter of 1944 there were counted 133 flights made by 125 planes in the Canary Islands). From Ifni (Western Africa Spanish territory), 13 shots were made. By nationalities, 35 American planes received fire from the Canary Islands, 8 from the United Kingdom and another 13 could not have their nationality verified.

The Spanish antiaircraft had to shoot in some cases to neutralize the aggressor aircraft batteries, although in many cases they shot only as a warning. On February 21, 1943, a Vickers Wellington was damaged by Spanish anti-aircraft artillery and had to make a forced landing several kilometers from Cabo Juby airfield. In June 1943 a 144 Sqdn of the British Coastal Command Bristol Beaufighter Mk.X was attacked by Spanish anti-aircraft batteries at Punta Malabata, near Tangier. The plane made an emergency landing, the pilot died and the observer was injured and subsequently captured. Also two French planes were hit by shrapnel from the firing of anti-aircraft artillery on April 15, 1944.

New diplomatic contacts maintained in the last quarter of 1944 with the British and American ambassadors, concluded that antiaircraft batteries would not fire on their planes when they flew over the sea (over Spanish territory, there was a risk of being shot). Anyway, the war was approaching to its end, so Spanish government determined that from December 1944, the Allied planes will not be fired even if they flew over Spanish territory (with the exception that these flights were repeatedly and provocatively made). Finally, from the last days of April 1945, it was decided that planes that passed over the Canary Islands airspace will not be fired any more.

Air Incidents With Axis Aircraft

The incidents with planes belonging to the Axis were not very frequent, and took place with French aircraft. This was motivated by the fact that France and Spain shared many kilometers of borders and jurisdictional waters in North Africa. From the "Operation Torch", incidents increased in number due to the existence of aircraft from many nationalities close to the Protectorate Spanish airspace.

North-West Africa witnessed another shot down of a Spanish aircraft by an aircraft of a belligerent country. On February 5, 1941, a Spanish Ju-52/3m transport aircraft carried out its tasks from the Sidi-Ifni aerodrome (belonging to the African Atlantic coast Spanish territory) to the Spanish mainland. In this case the attacking planes were two French fighters and attacked it on the sea 30 km from Casablanca. The Ju-52/3m was damaged and had to land in Rabat, belonging to French Morocco.

Also in various sources are mentioned some skirmishes between Spanish Group 27 He-112 B aircraft based in North Africa (in Nador) and France Vichy Dewoitine 520 aircraft (and therefore allies of Germany) based in Port Lyautey (Morocco). Fortunately there were not more Spanish aircraft shot down in these clashes over North African skies.

The Russian Front: The Blue Squadron

For this part of the text, we have used several information sources, highlighting the exceptional and superb texts by Juan Arráez Cerdá, Jorge Fernández-Coppel Larrinaga, Carlos Caballero Jurado and Francisco Martínez Canales.

We have already commented the political situation of Spain during the years of the WW2, so in this chapter, without further delay, we will narrate the participation of Spanish pilots in the world conflict. The winning side in the SCW commanded by General Franco, was evidently close to the German (after the aid of both Germany and Italy in the Spanish conflict) so after the German invasion of the USSR in 1941, as well as the organization of The Blue Division, the Blue Squadron was also created to provide air support to its Blue Division compatriots who fought in the north of the USSR (a fact that would never come to true since the Spanish air unit remained in central Russia, despite the requests of the Spanish Government to be added to the Blue Division). This decision was made at the last moment as Blue Division initial location was also the Central sector, which caused some upset among the volunteers. The Expeditionary Squadron should be the equivalent of a Luftwaffe Staffel, although it was not like a Staffel in reality.

Apart from an emotional explanation (the return to combat against communism as it had been done in the SCW but now returning the visit to the Soviets), the Blue Squadron was born due to different interests that the Spanish Government raised:

on the one hand a political explanation and on the other a practical or learning explanation.

The political explanation was that with the birth of the Blue Squadron, the support that was given to the Franco´s National Army with the Legion Condor during the SCW years was returned to Germany.

During the SCW, the National Aviation had learned a lot from its Italian comrades and especially from the Germans. One of the aspects that were assimilated by the newly created EdA to impose them on their Blue Squadron was the rotation of the pilots. The pilots of the Legion Condor were rotated every time period with the intention that the maximum number of pilots could take part in the SCW and therefore accelerate their learning and handling of modern aircraft. In the same way, the Spanish Expeditionary Squadron acted during its participation in WW2 within the Luftwaffe. For this reason we should not really talk about the Blue Squadron, but about the Blue Squadrons, since there were 5 Spanish squadrons that fought in the Russian skies throughout their stay on the Eastern front between September 1941 and March 1944 approximately, every six months a Squadron was relieved with the following one.

Being a unit about the size of a Staffel, they were assigned throughout their period of service on Luftwaffe´s Jagdgeschwader 27 and 51. A German Staffel initially had nine aircraft commanded by an officer. After the first months of the war, the number of aircraft assigned to each Staffel rose to 12-20 aircraft. Three or four Staffel formed a Gruppe, and three or four Gruppe formed a Jagdgeschwader (Wing). The number of pilots varied from 20 to 25 and ground personnel varied between 80 and 150, therefore each group was made up of about 40-50 aircraft and about 500 men. Pilots also performed secondary tasks on the ground, such as supervising aircraft maintenance tasks, communication, etc.

The 5 Squadrons operated in the USSR without having any relationship with their comrades in the Blue Division, since their actions were developed in the Army Group Center sector during such important moments as the German offensive on Moscow or the battles of Kharkov, Smolensko and Kursk.

As happened with the Blue Division, a lot of volunteers wanted to "return the visit" to the Soviets, to form the Blue Squadron. As it is reasonable to think, unlike what happened in the Blue Division, the Blue Squadron volunteers were all members of the EdA. The EdA pilots were usually as well prepared as their German comrades (we must always remember that a very important differentiating element was that while the Luftwaffe pilots flew modern aircraft, the EdA pilots did so in airplanes that were mostly obsolete in the 1941 Europe). This was motivated because many of the Spanish pilots that had flown with their German comrades of the Condor Legion in 1936-39, had often piloted similar aircraft and knew and dominated German tactics.

The practical or learning explanation of the Blue Squadron borning was to collect as much knowledge and training as possible by being part of the powerful Luftwaffe. In this way, all this information could be used to improve the performance of the EdA. This fact was the one that really motivated that relays were constituted for the pilots and the expeditionary personnel after six months of stay in the front. After all, the Blue Squadron copied the operating mode of the Legion Condor during the SCW.

The missions carried out by the Spanish squadrons in Russia were generally of four different types:

- Free Hunt Missions (Freie Jagd): they were the most suitable missions for the fighter pilots and the most desired ones as well. There were many victories that were achieved with this type of missions.

- Ground attack missions: these were about damaging the enemy ground forces as much as possible. The pilots of the 1st Squadron participated in numerous missions of this type, although this was not normal because they belonged to a Fighter unit. Many of the Spanish pilots who participated in the SCW had carried out missions of this type and were able to carry them out successfully.

- Escort missions: in them, the airplanes had to give protection to bombers formations, attack planes or reconnaissance aircraft. These missions had the added difficulty of the lower speed that the escorted aircraft had in many cases with respect to the fighters. They required a strict flight formations command and being very attentive to the appearance of enemy aircraft.

- Alert or alarm missions: they were always ready to take off two planes with their pilots in the cockpit. On occasion there were four planes on alert. These airplanes had to be prepared during most of the hours of the day, varying according to the light and weather conditions.

1st Squadron

The 1st Squadron was officially formed on July 14, 1941 in Madrid and was under the command of the commander Angel Salas Larrazabal, with his second commander José Muñoz Jiménez (he was actually the man appointed to command the 2nd Blue Squadron, but had managed to join the 1st Blue Squadron as a learning mode). Under his orders he had 16 pilots (15 belonging to the Squadron and Major Muñoz) and 78 officers, NCOs and service and mechanical soldiers, bringing the total number of men to 125. The ground echelon was commanded by Commander Ramón Salas Larrazábal, brother of Commander Angel Salas Larrazabal, the head of the 1st Squadron.

The commander Ángel Salas Larrazabal was a very expert pilot who commanded the 2nd Morato Group Squadron during the SCW, participating in 618 missions and 49 air combats, achieving 17 shot down planes and 48 vehicles destroyed on

Lieutenant Fernando Sánchez-Arjona y Courtoy of the 4th Blue Squadron that managed 9 Soviet planes shot down. He died on November 9, 1943 due to the formation of ice on his plane wings when he was taking off from the Orscha airfield. [Courtesy of Juan Arráez Cerdá]

Lieutenant José Ramón Gavilán of the 3rd Blue Squadron has just taken over one of the Bf 109 F-2 "Zacutos" of the 2nd Squadron, which gave to the 3rd Blue Squadron 10 Bf 109 F-2 in good conditions for the flight and 4 in repair. In the background the German Fw 190 that shared the airfield with the Spaniards. [Courtesy of Juan Arráez Cerdá]

After the Oath to the Führer for the fight against communism of the 4th Blue Squadron at the Toulouse-Colomiers Air Base (in occupied France), the Spanish officers chat with the Germans with the Fw 190 with whom they have trained at the background.
[Courtesy of Juan Arráez Cerdá]

Commander Mariano Cuadra Medina of the 4th Blue Squadron has just returned from a service in which he has achieved a new victory. In total, their confirmed that 10 Soviet planes were shot down: 6 LaGG-3, 2 Il-2, one LaGG-5 and one Bell P-39 (from the aid that USA delivered to the USSR). There he won the 2nd Class Iron Cross and the Spanish Military Medal.
[Courtesy of Juan Arráez Cerdá]

Commander Javier Murcia, 5th Blue Squadron chief testing one of the Messerschmitt Bf 109 G that they just handed over to replace the Fw 190 A-3 that were flying.
[Courtesy of Juan Arráez Cerdá]

Oath to the Führer for the fight against communism of the 5th Blue Squadron in Toulouse/Colomiers. [Courtesy of Juan Arráez Cerdá]

In this picture we see Lieutenant Hermenegildo Menéndez "Paco el Minero" and Aviation Land Troops Lieutenant Fernando Tomé with Blue Division nurses. [Courtesy of Juan Arráez Cerdá]

Three Messerschmitt Bf-109 B-2 of the Legion Condor. These initial models of the famous German fighter used by the Spaniards during the SCW, made it easier for Spaniards to learn how to handle more modern models such as the E or F. [Courtesy of Asisbiz]

This is the liaison Ju 52 that piloted by "Paco el Minero" was shot down by Soviet guerrillas fire. [Courtesy of Juan Arráez Cerdá]

The obsolete seaplane Dornier Wal, was used by Spain during WW2 in the 51 Squadron in the Northern Africa Spanish Protectorate. [Courtesy of Military Modeling and History]

Mechanics belonging to the 5th Blue Squadron next to one of their Fw 190 A-3. This Squadron could only be in service for about a month. [Courtesy of Juan Arráez Cerdá]

Italian torpedo that was recovered intact in the beach of La Línea de la Concepción (Cádiz) after being launched against Gibraltar by Italian torpedo planes in 1941. This torpedo is currently preserved in the Army Museum of Seville. [Photograph of the author]

Spain made Cr.32 with the name of Hispano HA.132L. This aircraft had been completely obsolete since the beginning of WW2. [Free from Public Domain by Alan Wilson]

The Dornier Wal seaplane, despite its obsolescence, remained in service for several years in Spain. In 1945, 5 of them were still in service. In the seaplane of the photograph we can clearly see the tricolor badge. [Courtesy of Military Modeling and History]

Photograph of a Heinkel He-111 E-1. This type of aircraft had already been outdated after the introduction of later models, mainly H. [Free from Public Domain by Estrelas from Vigo]

Photograph of two Italian made CANT Z.506 B seaplanes in 1939 at the seaplanes base in Pollensa. From the Baleares Islands, Spanish aviation controlled much of the western Mediterranean. [Free from Public Domain]

Wrecks of TQ + MU He-111H-23 in La Concha beach (San Sebastián) observed by a multitude of people. This plane came from Norway and it was where Leon Degrelle was traveling, fleeing the capture by the Allies. [Free from Public Domain by Vicente Martín-Fondo Car-Kutxa Fototeka]

Joaquín García Morato, leader of national fighter branch during the SCW. In the tail of the plane we can see the emblem of the Patrulla Morato (Morato Patrol) with its motto "Vista, suerte y al toro". [Courtesy of Almena]

Close-up of the sentence written in the Bf 109 F2 Black 1 belonging to the 2nd Blue Squadron in tribute to Captain Noriega died on July 1, 1942. We can read " CAPITÁN NORIEGA ¡Presente!" (CAPTAIN NORIEGA Among us!). [Courtesy of Asisbiz]

A Messerschmitt Bf 109 E belonging to the 15. (span)/JG 27 taxing in the Staritsa airstrip in October 1941. We can see the 1st Blue Squad badge in the nose of the fighter, that is painted in yellow. [Courtesy of Asisbiz]

Photograph of one Fw 200 C Kondor. Many of these planes flew in maritime missions and were shot down or forced to make forced landings in Spain. [Bundesarchiv Bild 146-1978-043-02]

Salas Larrazabal Fiat Cr.32 from Group 2-G-3 2nd Squadron of during the SCW. In the tail of the plane we can see the emblem of the Patrulla Morato. [Courtesy of Military Modeling and History]

88 mm anti-aircraft gun similar to those that Germany sold to Spain during WW2 for the protection of Spanish skies against Allied aircraft. [Free from Public Domain by Ramon Piñeiro]

This Fiat G.50 fighter shows us one of the important defect: the landing gear. These aircraft suffered various problems in the landing gear during their service in North Africa, so they flew less hours than the He 112 based in Nador too. [Courtesy of Juan Arráez Cerdá]

In 1940 the Spanish Air Force had 44 obsolete He 51 in the 31st Regiment based on the Getafe airbase (Madrid). This attack aircraft, as the one in the photograph, had previously been used during the SCW. [Courtesy of Military Modeling and History]

Nice photograph of a Fiat Cr.32 in 1939. You can see on its wing the Spanish Aviation tricolor badge, the St. Andrew´s Cross on the tail and black circle in the fuselage. Although obsolete, the Cr.32 was the fighter that the Air Force disposed of in greater numbers. [Courtesy of Military Modeling and History]

Several Cr.32 escorting an S.81 during the SCW. After the SCW the S.81 was deployed by the 1st Air Brigade of the Cantabrico Air Region. [Courtesy of Military Modeling and History]

In 1944 Germany sold 12 modern seaplanes Do 24 T-3 for maritime rescue missions. In this photo we see a Do 24 T-3 preserved today. [Free from Public Domain by Curimedia]

This was the fate of many Luftwaffe and Allied aircraft in Spanish jurisdictional waters. Although in this case it is a KG 40 Fw 200 C Kondor sank in the Atlantic Ocean west of Ireland. [Public domain]

Close-up of the 2nd Blue Squadron badge composed by the emblem of the Joaquín García Morato Fighter Group on a red cross of Santiago in the nose of a Bf 109 F4, belonging to the 15. (span.)/JG 51. [Courtesy of Asisbiz]

The Lavochkin LaGG-3 was one of the Soviet fighters that Spanish pilots frequently encountered in the skies of the USSR. 58 LaGG-3 were shot down by the pilots of the 2nd, 3rd and 4th Blue Squadrons. [Courtesy of Asisbiz]

Several Fw 190 of JG 51 in a snowy airstrip in Russia during the winter of 1942. The 3rd and 4th Blue Squadrons disposed of this modern German fighter. [Courtesy of Asisbiz]

Painted by Arkadiusz Wróbel

Focke Wulf Fw 190 A2

White 5 of 15.(span.)/JG 51, 4th Escuadrilla Azul, flown by Ensign Luis Chicharro Lamamié de Clairac, Orel/USSR, August 1943. The aircraft carries the yellow theater band in the fuselage, yellow undercowling, underside of the wing tips and black and yellow spinner. On August 21, Alférez Chicharro (who just arrived only 9 days before to Russia) in his second war mission was shot down during a dogfight against several LaGG-3s, LaGG-5s and Yak 9s. The missions carried out by the Spanish squadrons in Russia were of different kind: free hunt (Freie Jagd), ground attack and escort missions mainly. At least two planes with their pilots in the cockpit were always ready to take off. (sometimes there were four planes on alert). These airplanes had to be prepared during most of the hours of the day, varying according to the light and weather conditions.

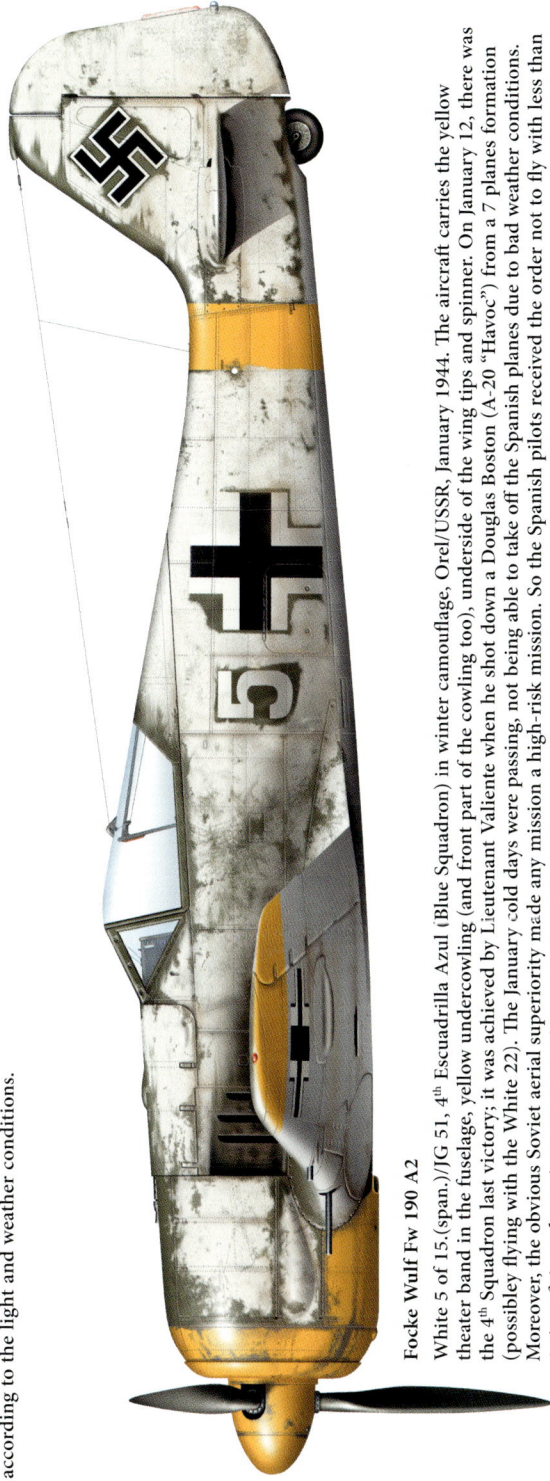

Focke Wulf Fw 190 A2

White 5 of 15.(span.)/JG 51, 4th Escuadrilla Azul (Blue Squadron) in winter camouflage, Orel/USSR, January 1944. The aircraft carries the yellow theater band in the fuselage, yellow undercowling (and front part of the cowling too), underside of the wing tips and spinner. On January 12, there was the 4th Squadron last victory; it was achieved by Lieutenant Valiente when he shot down a Douglas Boston (A-20 "Havoc") from a 7 planes formation (possibley flying with the White 22). The January cold days were passing, not being able to take off the Spanish planes due to bad weather conditions. Moreover, the obvious Soviet aerial superiority made any mission a high-risk mission. So the Spanish pilots received the order not to fly with less than 4 aircraft in order to increase protection.

Painted by Arkadiusz Wróbel

Messerschmitt Bf 109 G6

White 2 of 15.(span.)/JG 51, 5th Escuadrilla Azul (Blue Squadron) in winter camouflage. Bobruisk airfield/USSR, February 1944. The aircraft carries the yellow theater band in the fuselage, yellow undercowling and yellow underside of the wing tips and spinner. The 5th Escuadrilla Azul was the only one Spanish Squadron that managed to pilot the Bf 109 G6, but only had almost one month of service within the Luftwaffe. The pilots belonging to the 5th Blue Squadron carried out 86 flight missions, participating in 6 clashes against Soviet planes and not credited any shot down; however they suffered the loss of one pilot.

Messerschmitt Bf 109 F2

Black 12 of 15.(span.)/JG 51, 2nd Escuadrilla Azul (Blue Squadron) in winter camouflage. Orel/USSR, Winter 1942. The aircraft carries almost full Eastern Front markings: yellow theater band in the fuselage, yellow undercowling and yellow underside of the wing tips but spinner is in winter camouflage. The white paint was applied in varying densities, indeed the top of the yellow undercowling. The 2nd Escuadrilla Azul was formed on February 6, 1942 in Morón (in Seville) and was comanded by Comandante (major or commander) Julio Salvador Díaz-Benjumea; a great prestige officer that achieved 23 air victories and a downed balloon during the Spanish Civil War.

the ground; and being shot down 4 times. He was the perfect boss for the 1ˢᵗ Blue Squadron that would then have to transmit all the knowledge learned in combat for the Spanish EdA.

The 1ˢᵗ Squadron left Madrid for Berlin on July 24, 1941. The journey to its destination in Berlin was by train and took 3 days. They left the Estación del Norte (Madrid), arrived in San Sebastián, Irún, Hendaye (already in France, where they were received with great honors). As anecdotal data, when they left Hendaye towards Paris, the Spaniards were ordered to return to Hendaye to be disinfected of exanthematic typhus by distrusting the health status of any person from Spain.

The arrival in Berlin came three days after the departure, on July 27. In spite of the combat experience of the Spanish pilots, when arriving at German land they were sent to the Jagdfliegerschule 1 in Werneuchen, 28 kilometers away from Berlin. They were received with a music band that played the Spanish anthem (but the one of the Republic that had been defeated in the SCW), which gave rise to some upset in the Spaniards.

They spent three months in Werneuchen receiving instruction to carry out joint missions with the Luftwaffe pilots. Needless to say, this long period of instruction did not please the expert and veteran Spanish pilots (among the 17 Spanish pilots, they had 79 air victories during the SCW, and Commander Salas and Captain Aristides had 17 aircraft shot down each, 11 shot down Captain Bayo, 7 Captain Allende, 7 Lieutenant Ibarreche, 6 Lieutenant O'Connor, 5 Lieutenant Alcocer, 5 Lieutenant Cesteros, 3 Lieutenant Lacour and 1 Lieutenant Ruibal).

On July 29, the pilots' training plan was notified and training flights began with Bf 109 D and Bf 109 F. During the training period, the Spanish pilots were divided according to their greater or lesser knowledge of Bf 109 management: a group formed by knowledgeable Bf 109 pilots, another pilots group who knew the Bf 109 but had flown little with them and a third pilots group who did not know the flight with the Bf 109. The pilots with less knowledge in the Bf 109 were trained with Arado Ar 96 aircraft. The days passed tediously and the Spaniards wanted to start their combat actions as quickly as possible, but the German organization was slower.

On August 16, they took the allegiance oath in the Werneuchen training camp (like their comrades in the Blue Division, the men of the Blue Squadron swore with the usual oath used by the Germans but specifying that only "in the fight against communism "). It is important to emphasize that the Spaniards who fought against the USSR in a general way did it against the communism and not for that reason means that they shared Nazi ideology with their German comrades (neither the Spaniards were generally of Nazi ideology or all the German military were Nazis).

It was shortly after, during the training when Commander Salas was informed that the Spanish Squadron was not going to act as a fighter squadron, but mainly as a ground attack squadron. The cause was the Wehrmacht's need for the Luftwaffe´s support in the attack against the USSR vastness.

A curiosity is the fact that all the pilots from the 1st Blue Squadron were officers. In the Luftwaffe (according to Caballero) it was not usual to see a captain in command of a Schwarm, but of the whole Squadron or even of a Gruppe.

On September 5, the Squadron receives its first combat aircraft: 12 Messerschmitt Bf 109E-7/B called by the Spaniards "Tripalas (three bladed propeller)" (during the training period the rumors that had in Werneuchen said that it could possibly be the new model F that the Spaniards would use, but it was not like that). Remember that during the SCW, this model of aircraft was already used in Spain and was fast and maneuvering (therefore, it was much appreciated by its pilots). Finally, the 1st Squadron, once the training period was completed, was ready to be sent to the front and with its planes ready to take off.

The ground staff (ground echelon) left on September 22 towards its destination on the Eastern front. On the 26th the pilots took off with their airplanes to their destination on two stop offs, the first was an airfield in Minsk (although the idea was to be there for a week, on the 30th they took off to their final aerodrome: Moschna). Only 11 aircraft landed in Minsk, as the Bf 109 piloted by Commander Muñoz had to make a forced landing that caused minor damage to the plane. On the 30th 7 squadron's planes took off to their second stop off (the other 4 stayed in Minsk to be checked), to finally land at the aerodrome from where they would begin to carry out their missions: the Moschna airfield (northwest of Smolensk).

The Moschna airfield was a typical close to the front airfield since it had no facilities and the airstrip was the field. The staff of the Luftwaffe had to seek refuge in huts on many occasions shared with the peasants and so it happened to those men who wore the German uniform and a Spanish emblem on the right shoulder.

The Spanish Squadron was incorporated with the denomination of "15 Spanische Staffel" to the Luftflotte 2. VIII Fliegerkorps Jagdgeschwader 27; its official denomination was 15.(span.)/JG 27 and was assigned to the command of Major Woldenga. Despite belonging to the JG 27 that was a Fighter Geschwader, the Blue Squadron operated as an autonomous unit within the ground attack group II(S)LG2, which was under the command of Major Otto Weiss. The 15.(span.)/JG 27 was structured in 3 Patrols with 5 aircraft each and the Stab:

Stab: Chief: commander Ángel Salas. Second commander: Commander José Muñoz.

1st Patrol: Captain Arístides García, and Lieutenants Alfonso Ruibal, Ángel Mendoza, Ricardo Bartolomé and Abundio Cesteros.

2nd Patrol: Captain Javier Allende, and Lieutenants Luis Alcocer, José Lacour, Javier Busquets and Alfonso Gracia-Rodríguez.

3rd Patrol: Captain Carlos Bayo and Lieutenants Esteban Ibarreche, Emilio O'Connor, Manuel Kindelán and Demetrio Zorita.

As we can see, all the Spanish pilots were officers, a fact that attracted enough attention to their colleagues in the Luftwaffe.

The Blue Squadron used an emblem on its planes, a white circle with three birds in the middle (a hawk, a bustard and a blackbird) and the phrase "Vista, suerte y al toro" that means "Sight, luck and 'nut up' "(which was the motto of the Escuadilla García Morato during the SCW and came from the bullfighting world) and the number II (in Roman).

At that time the German Army was preparing its final blow against the city of Moscow in the so-called "Operation Taifun" (started on September 30). This German attack had led to the formation of Soviet resistance Pockets between Smolensk and Viazma.

The first mission in which Spanish pilots took part was carried out on October 2, coinciding with the start of "Operation Taifun". The 23 individual outings that took place on October 2 were to escort the Henschel Hs 123 and Bf 109 who made ground attacks against the Soviet troops in the Orel area. That same day, the 1st Squadron suffered its first casualty, when, after completing an escort mission to Hs 123, Salas, Ruibal, Alcocer and Allende entered combat with a formation of 22 MiG-3, several Polikarpov I-16s and several DB-3 bombers. Despite the clash between the Soviet and Spanish planes, there was no loss in any flight formation; but Lieutenant Alcocer became disoriented by running out of fuel (he had been flying for more than an hour) and tried to make an emergency landing, during which he took out the wheels and died in the collision with the collimator of his plane (a standard for forced landings was never to unfold the wheels and remove the collimator).

The body of Lieutenant Alcocer was transferred to Werneuchen in a Ju 52, which on the return trip to Moschna, picked up Major Muñoz who was still in Minsk due to the failure of his plane.

The air support of the Luftwaffe in the offensive against Moscow fell on 1300 aircraft mainly belonging to the Kesselring's 2nd LuftFlotte. The Fighter units that participated were the JG 51 (with 4 Groups), the JG 27 (with 2 Groups and the 1st Blue Squadron) and two Fighter Groups from JG 3 and JG 53.

On October 3, the 4 planes that had been left in Minsk (piloted by Captain Bayo and Lieutenants O'Connor, Mendoza and Kindelán) and the ground echelon troops (who had departed by train on 22 September) arrived in Moschna. On the same day the 1st Squadron made 6 close air support and ground attack missions. In one of them, Commander Salas destroyed several trucks of a Soviet convoy. The first congratulations from Major Weiss to the Spanish Squadron were received by Commander Salas. The Spanish pilots participated in attacks against ground targets in the battle of Vyazma-Briansk and later supported the left side of the German advance against Moscow.

On October 4 during one of the Squadron missions, three Spanish aircraft (one of them piloted by Commander Salas) watched 2 Petlyakov Pe-2. Commander Salas managed to shoot down one of them firing his machine guns and cannons. Shortly after, Commander Salas and his wingman attacked an I-16 that was trying to attack several Hs 123; the result was that the Soviet plane crashed due to the flight maneuvers it carried out. On the same day, several Soviet convoys were machine-gunned on the ground.

On October 5 and due to the Spanish pilots great bravery and courage with their commander flying many of the combat missions, General Richtofen (who was in the SCW in the Legion Condor) visited the Spaniards and granted the commander Salas the 2ⁿᵈ Class Iron Cross.

On the 6ᵗʰ, Commander Salas again shot down another enemy plane (a MiG-3) in another escort mission to the ground attack aircraft belonging to II(S)LG2.

The advance of the Wehrmacht caused that the frontline was very far from the Moschna airbase, reason why the 1ˢᵗ Squadron was transferred to the aerodrome in Bjeloj (to the north and near Orel, which ended up being conquered by the Germans). On the 7th, 8 planes flew to Bjeloj in two Patrols, suffering damage when one of the planes landed. This airstrip was in even worse condition than that of Moschna (the ground was very muddy) although the Spaniards were only there for 4 days, during which a new Bf 109 for the Squadron arrived, piloted by Lieutenant Lacour (who replaced the damaged Spanish aircraft). In the three days that they were able to carry out missions (on the 9ᵗʰ the bad weather prevented the planes from taking off), the Spaniards flew 62 times but without shooting down enemy planes. On the 10th, Commander Muñoz (who had suffered the first aircraft squadron´s trouble) joined to his comrades flying in a Ju 52 piloted also by Spaniards.

They moved from the Bjeloj airfield to the Konaja airfield, which was nothing more than an empty ground strip near a forest and a village. Again there was no infrastructure to accommodate the Spaniards, who on October 12 had to set up their tents despite the intense cold. On the 12ᵗʰ, 6 planes arrived at Konaja at first; hours later another 2 planes arrived. In Bjeloj, two planes remained in repair and pilots Kindelán and Ruibal flew in a Ju 52 to Warsaw to pick up 2 new planes.

Already from its new base, on the 13ᵗʰ the missions of the Spaniards resumed. During a reconnaissance mission on Kalinin (Tver), 4 Bf 109 Spaniards saw 3 I-16. Commander Salas constantly attacked one of them with such aggression that the Soviet pilot crashed to the ground. Later in another encounter with several MiG-3, Captain Bayo managed to land one of the enemies. That same day, a biplane was shot down by Lieutenant Ibarreche. In one day 3 enemy planes had been shot down, which made the 13ᵗʰ day the most successful one for the Spaniards until that day.

They were starting to win their first combats against the retreating Soviets, since a few hours later the city of Kalinin was occupied by the Germans.

On October 14 during a Free Hunt mission (Freie Jagd), 4 Bf 109 Spaniards located 3 DB-3, which they attacked. The result was the 3 Soviet aircraft shot down (two by Salas and one by Bayo). Shortly after, Commander Salas received the visit of Marshal Kesserling, who was the head of the Luftflote, to congratulate the Spaniards.

On the 15th the bad weather prevented the flight of the Spaniards, and the next day they received the order to move to the recently conquered Kalinin. This fact motivated the Spanish base was very close to the front line.

The first mission was to escort the Ju 52s that transported part of the 1st Blue Squadron ground echelon. This was motivated by the combat front proximity and therefore of Soviet aviation. On October 16, the first 7 Spanish aircraft arrived at its new aerodrome and soon after, two more aircraft did so. A few days later 3 more aircraft joined, so the Squadron was back to full (although part of the ground echelon that had not been moved in Ju 52, was still on the way). This fact is important, since we have been able to see how during several days of fighting in which the Spaniards had participated, in most of the occasions they had to do it without having the whole ground echelon (with the difficulties of fly a plane without all the ground crewtaking care of it).

The new Spanish airbase was attacked on October 17 by Soviet tanks. This attack was stopped thanks to the quick intervention of the Hs 123 and Bf 109 that made them retreat after destroying a tank. This is a good example to demonstrate the proximity of the airbase to the front, but also the Soviet aviation (the VVS) made several attacks against the Spanish base. In one of them, on the 18th, Commander Salas and Lieutenant Lacour managed to take off when they were being machine-gunned on the ground; managing to repel the Soviet I-16 and DB-3. During that same day, Lieutenant Lacour shot down a DB-3 and Lieutenant Garcia-Rodriguez possibly an I-16 (not confirmed).

The proximity of the Soviets motivated that on Sunday the 19th Major Otto Weiss (the commander of the II(S)LG 2) ordered the alert status for pilots and ground echelon. From that moment and before an imminent Soviet attack, they had to be in charge of the defense of the aerodrome in an urban area next to the railroad between Leningrad and Moscow. As it was suspected, the Soviet attack took place but by another zone different from where the Spaniards were; even capturing part of Kalinin. On October 21 two Spanish Bf 109 were destroyed on ground after a Soviet attack, since they were very close to the Spanish base. The next day, German reinforcements arrived, temporarily re-establishing the front line and securing it. In addition, the Squadron received ammunition and fuel so it was ready to fly again.

In the face of the enemy, the Hs 123 biplanes punished the Soviets again and again with their ground attacks while the Blue Squadron planes escorted them. One of the Spaniards (who knew the Hs 123, who also piloted in Spain) came to fly one of these biplanes and collaborated with his German comrades.

The non-stop Germans and Spaniards fighting in this front sector along with the effective organization of the defense (thanks to Major Weiss orders) prevented the Spanish base from being fenced off, earned him the decoration of the Oak Leaves for his Iron Cross Knight's Cross.

To stop the enemy planes wave attacking the Kalinin airfield, the Spaniards were ordered to attack the Soviet airbase in Klin (from where many of these air attacks came). The Blue Squadron pilots attacked the Klin base twice, managing to destroy 2 Mig-3s on the ground and damaging a biplane in flight (in the first attack), having to retreat later before the arrival of 18 Mig-3s. In the second attack, which took place in the afternoon, the Soviets were alert, which prevented new successes from the Spaniards.

On October 27, Klin was attacked again at dawn without great success, but a train that was circulating along the Leningrad-Moscow line was machine-gunned and damaged. In the afternoon the attack was repeated with 5 Bf 109, Captain Bayo destroying a Mig-3 that was taking off. The effective antiaircraft artillery prevented the Spanish pilots from achieving new victories in Klin although on returning Commander Salas managed to shoot down a DB-3. During the return flight Lieutenant Ruibal had problems with the engine, which caused him to separate from his companions and finally get lost. There was no more news of the brave pilot.

During all the combats the Blue Squadron had belonged to the II(S)LG2, but this unit was sent to rearguard after the Kalinin combats. This motivated that the Spaniards were dependent of the JG 52, although its official denomination continued being the one of 15.(span.)/JG 27. In spite of it, the Spaniards continued carrying out ground attack missions. In particular, they tried to destroy (with little success) several artillery batteries that harassed the Germans in Kalinin. The situation was critical in the front, which was a few meters from the airfield that was constantly hammered by the Soviet artillery, so on October 30 the Blue Squadron was finally ordered to transfer to an airfield in Starica or Staritza. The transfer was made with the Bf 109s, Ju 52s and by road and was carried out over several days. On October 31, Commander Salas received the First Class Iron Cross.

During October the Squadron operated successively from Moschna, Bjeloj, Konaja, Kalinin and Staritza; getting to shoot down 10 enemy planes but suffering the losses of a dead pilot, a missing one and a third who was injured.

In its new base, bad weather and ice made maintenance and flight tasks difficult. Despite this, on November 4, Commander Salas and Lieutenant Ibarreche piloted a Free Hunt mission. In the course of the mission they faced 3 MiG-3 without being able to shoot down any of them, but Major Salas' plane was damaged causing him to make an emergency landing. Fortunately Salas was not injured and was able to return with his Squadron.

After several days in Staritza, the Squadron was ordered to move to Rusa (80 kilometers from Moscow) on November 12, to participate in the offensive against Moscow. Only 6 aircraft arrived in Rusa, as the wear and inadequate maintenance due to bad weather and continuous fighting had left the squadron with half of its aircraft. Although the runway was better than the ones of the previous aerodromes, the accommodation of men was still quite inadequate. The bad weather and the cold (up to 25° below zero) prevented new flights of the Spaniards until November 11 when the two planes that were in the Alarm status (with their pilots inside the cockpit ready to take off) had to take off to intercept a Ilyushin Il-2 flight formation attacking the Spanish airbase. Only Major Salas' plane managed to take off and damage one of the Il-2's (possibly knocked it down as two German pilots confirmed, although it was not finally recorded as a victory). The other plane on Alarm status could not take off due to mechanical problems at the last moment.

On the 13th, attack missions against Soviet airfields were carried out in Nekoliskoje and Jubiskoje, but without any victory to add. On the 14th, three Spanish planes carried out an escort mission to two-engine Bf 110s. That same day, at last, the ground echelon arrived at the Rusa base and Spanish pilots flew in the vicinity of Moscow.

Meanwhile, on November 15, the attack against Moscow second phase began. At the northeast of Moscow, the Blue Squadron was supporting the German troops against the Kalinin front XXX Soviet Army.

In the following days a lot of missions coincided with the German attacks destined to capture Moscow. During these days a Soviet Po-2 was destroyed on the ground on the 18th by Commander Salas while escorting several Hs 123. To increase the number of Spanish aircraft on the 17th, two Spanish pilots (Captain Bayo and Lieutenant Busquets) flew to Warsaw on a Ju 52 to pick up two planes for the Squadron.

The days 20, 21 and 22 the Spanish could not fly due to the heavy fog that prevented it. On the evening of November 23, German troops managed to conquer Kalinin. During the previous week the Luftwaffe (and therefore the Blue Squadron) had to fly from airstrips very close to the combat front and sometimes to shot distance from the Soviet artillery. On the 25th the Blue Squadron received 3 Messerschmitt ceded by a German Squadron.

On the 27th, numerous combat missions were carried out by the Spanish northeast of Klin; as ground attacks or escort tasks to Hs 123. The main tasks were the escort of both Ju 87 (who attacked the Moscow road 10-15 kilometers from Solnetschnogorsk) and Hs 123 (who attacked about 5 kilometers northeast of Istra). Both attack formations were received with an important fire of the Soviet antiaircraft artillery. That day Major Muñoz's plane was damaged by antiaircraft artillery while escorting the Hs 123 and had to bail out, although due to the low altitude the parachute was not fully deployed. Nothing was learned of the fate of the Spanish pilot despite the fact that a 4 Spanish aircraft Patrol with Salas in command took off to look for Commander Muñoz. The Squadron suffered a very important casualty, as it was one of the bravest and most capable pilots of all National Aviation during the SCW.

The following day, the Squadron moved to its new base in Klin (which the Spanish pilots knew well for having attacked it on numerous occasions), where they landed the 8 planes that the Spaniards had (same number as that of available pilots). This aerodrome was the closest to Moscow of all in which there was some Spanish Squadron. Two days after arriving at Klin, the Squadron was reinforced with another Bf 109 brought by Lieutenant Bartolomé.

On November 28, a Free Hunt mission was carried out in the Istra-Dimitrov area, where Lieutenants Mendoza and Lacour became disoriented and had to make an emergency landing about 200 kilometers away from Klin. Fortunately, the landing took place in the German zone and on December 3 they arrived safe at its aerodrome.

The missions were carried out day after day on the immense Soviet front. For example, on the 30th there were 6 Free Hunt missions, the Spaniards pliots flew in pairs in the Dimitrov-Ignatova zone (Moscow channel). The antiaircraft artillery fired the Luftwaffe planes, making very difficult accomplish any mission.

On December 2, on his third mission of the day, Lieutenant Allende machine-gunned an enemy plane. All the pilots carried out several missions every day, so the exhaustion was beginning to be noticed, but the German advance towards Moscow required a new effort from all the men. On December 4, a new loss occurred, when Lieutenant Bartolomé was shot down after being attacked by MiG-3 and Pe-2. It is possible that he managed to bail out, but the later Soviet ground forces advance prevented that the search of the Spanish pilot could be organized.

But the sign of the war was beginning to change and the Soviets not only resisted the Germans but also began to carry out attacks against them. On December 5 with temperatures about 35 degrees below zero, the German High Command gave orders to stop the offensive against Moscow but the battle in the sector continued, as the Russians had passed to the counterattack and the Army Group Center was forced to go on defensive positions. The Soviets managed to keep their aviation operatives, which began to harass the Luftwaffe, which could not get the planes operating due to the cold. The Klin airfield was very close to the battle front. That fact, along with the low temperatures motivated the decision to move the Blue Squadron to safer positions.

On December 6, the Soviet offensive began on the Moscow front, under Zhukov´s command. In the Kalinin area the Soviets managed to penetrate up to 10 kilometers through German lines, so the situation for the Germans and Spaniards changed drastically in just several days. It was necessary to retreat to defensive positions.

On the 8th again with intense cold, the Blue Squadron was preparing to retreat to Rusa. But the critical situation on the front due to the scarce German troops and the powerful Soviet advance, made the Spanish evacuation stop. The Soviets advanced towards Klin without opposition, and were only a few minutes from the German-Spanish base. Major Lessmann (Gruppe´s commodore) organized the defense of the base with the Blue Squadron, JG 52 1st Group and an anti-aircraft battery. Also, it was ordered to destroy the aircraft on ground if the Soviets approached (the Blue Squadron had only 4 Bf 109s left in flight conditions). Although it was tried to evacuate the Spaniards, the Soviets advance speed motivated that the Blue Squadron men were deployed forming a defensive line in a zone of the base (along with its German comrades). The Spanish force consisted of four platoons and HQ. Meanwhile, they tried to take off the 4 Bf 109s to evacuate them, but the ice on the wings and windshield prevented the flight; so that the four pilots were incorporated into the Spanish defensive formation, which consisted of 66 men in total. At dusk, the situation was critical and the blasting of the hangars was prepared if the Soviets approached the base.

Fortunately, at dawn on December 9 the situation was not so difficult although the base was attacked by the VVS without causing major damage and suffering a constant artillery fire. The idea was for the 4 Spanish planes to take off, but again it was impossible. A transport plane arrived at the base and began to evacuate some men. At dusk there were significant shootings near the airfield and the danger was greater again.

At dawn on the 10th, the situation was extremely risky at the aerodrome as Russian outposts were there. The Spanish planes tried again to take off, although one did not succeed and another had to return to land after takeoff. Both planes would be abandoned at the airfield, already with the Russian infantry attacking it. But the Soviet antiaircraft artillery only left that a Spanish airplane (adding all the Spanish and German airplanes of the aerodrome) piloted by Lieutenant Mendoza, arrived at its destination.

But the combats at the aerodrome continued and 2 Hs 123 managed to take off to attack the Soviets thanks to the help of the Spaniards. Despite the order not to land the transport aircraft for the evacuation (due to continuous gunfire against the base), during the day 2 Ju 52 landed and evacuated part of the Blue Squadron men.

Some German troops who came to the area managed to reduce the pressure that the Soviets exerted on the airfield. Thanks to that brief respite, Major Lessmann ordered that they had to repair the planes that were still in the airfield to try to evacuate them. He also gave the order that the Blue Squadron men be prepared for combat during the early hours of the morning. The Spaniards positioned themselves in a defensive position covered with snow but with little ammunition.

The situation as we can see was very tense during several days and nights in which the airfield was very close to being captured by the Soviets before the shortage of troops to defend them. Thanks to the Spanish Squadron pilots and the ground echelon men and the Luftwaffe unit with which they shared an airfield, which were "converted" into infantry soldiers, at dawn on December 12, part of the Klin airfield was still dominated by the Spaniards and Germans. At 08.30 am, the Spanish unit started walking to evacuate Klin to Nekrasino (15 kilometers from Klin). Only a soldiers team were left on the airfield with the mission to destroy the abandoned planes.

The Spanish column reached Nekrasino with great difficulties because of the cold and snow. On December 13 at dawn the column started to travel 12 more kilometers to reach Pavel'Cevo, being on the way bombarded by 6 Pe-2 aircraft (which did not cause significant damage). The Spaniards were completely exhausted but they spent the whole day and the night walking until the 14th, when they managed to get on several trucks that were going to Rusa. The Soviet aviation attacked them again (in this case I-16 that strafed them) causing several injuries. Finally the men managed to get to Rusa but in a bad shape after the several days of fighting and withdrawal on the snow they had lived (expert pilots and mechanics had been used as infantry and suffered enormous risks). On December 16, they were moved to Dugvino or Duguino (about 50 kilometers north of Wjasma) along with some vehicles and a Ju 52.

Already in Dugvino the Spaniards were waiting for new orders that would allow them to return to combat or if they would eventually be repatriated. During the evacuation Commander Salas did not know about the fate of the 7 men belonging to his Squadron, apart from the several wounded among the survivors. In the following days the men who had been left behind arrived (even Lieutenant Busquets arrived driving a Bf 109). While waiting for the orders, at least two Spanish pilots (Captain Allende and Lieutenant Zorita) piloted an Hs 123 of a German Squadron in support of the German troops because the Soviets approached Dugvino. On January 4 they were ordered to move to the Vitebsk aerodrome, where the Squadron was reorganized. In Dugvino the Spaniards met the German Ju 87 ace Hans Ulrich Rudel, who was there alongside with his Squadron. The Spaniards managed to gather 9 Bf 109s and they were ready again for combat, but they received the repatriation order on January 6, 1942. On February 11, the Squadron was ready to return to Spain, but before they were awarded several decorations, among which we must highlight the German Golden Cross received by Commander Salas.

On February 17 the Spaniards belonging to the Blue Squadron returned to Werneuchen, and on February 28 they were crossing the Spanish border. On March 1, they arrived at the Estación del Norte (Train Station) in Madrid, and were greeted with great joy by a crowd of people. The previous day, from that same Estación del Norte, the 2nd Blue Squadron had left for Germany. The 1st Blue Squadron was officially disbanded on March 4th.

Approximately after six months in combat the 1st Squadron returned to Spain, leaving in the USSR 5 pilots killed victims of the Soviet antiaircraft artillery or in accidents (commander Muñoz, Captain Arístides García López and lieutenants Alcocer, Ruibal and Bartolomé) and a soldier. For its part, the 1st Squadron carried out 422 combat missions, as bomber protection and Freie Jagd; and participated in 94 air combats managing to shoot down 10 confirmed enemy airplanes (six by Commander Salas Larrazabal, 2 shot down by Captain Bayo, 1 shot down by Lieutenant Lacour and 1 shot down by Lieutenant Ibarreche) and 4 not confirmed shots (commander Salas, captain Bayo, Captain García López and Lieutenant Mendoza), and also burning 5 planes on the ground (2 by Commander Salas, 1 by Lieutenant Cesteros, 1 by Lieutenant Zorita and 1 by Lieutenant Ibarreche). In addition to the aircraft shot down, we should highlight the numerous decorations and awards that received pilots as well as ground echelon men during the fighting months.

The 1st Squadron experienced multiple changes of aerodromes, bad weather, Soviet land offensives that forced the Squadron`s men to act as infantry. In addition, in many cases, the Squadron`s pilots could not have all the planes since, due to the repairs of the Bf 109 and the various base changes, many planes remained on the previous aerodrome waiting to be repaired to rejoin to the Squadron. For the same reason, the ground echelon in many cases went on difficult marches through the Soviet lands in search of its Squadron (so the planes had to be operational despite lacking an adequate infrastructure to be in flight). All these difficulties were not enough for the Spanish aircraft operability to be the maximum possible at every moment, even though on very few occasions the Squadron had all available aircraft (or pilots, who had to carry out several trips to pick up new planes for the Squadron).

The 1st Blue Squadron experience was considered very positive by Germany, due to its courageous performance on the Russian front. This general satisfaction can be seen in the ABC newspaper article in its edition of Andalusia on Wednesday, July 15, 1942:

Berlin 14. The relief of the Spanish aviators who make up the glorious Blue Squadron provides the opportunity for the Berlin newspaper "Volkischer Beobachter" to write, in a vibrant article, the heroic performance of this squadron in its fight against communism on the Russian front.

The newspaper reminds, organ of the German National Socialist Party, the famous motto of the García Morato squad: "Vista, suerte y al toro"; and under which the Blue Squadron also fights, and praises the Spanish aviators "ace", who after endless feats during the crusade, saw his life truncated in an Aviation accident, shortly after achieving Franco's victory.

"The Blue Squadron was created when the Blue Division was organized, and under the command of Commander Salas, they demonstrated their mastery of the air during

last winter's fight. The victories they got are testimony that the Blue Squadron retains the old combative spirit of García Morato's Squadron, and their losses increase, once again, their fame. "

"Today, "the" continues Volkischer Beobachter", "the second Blue Squadron is ready to enter combat. It is also made up of the best Spanish fighter pilots, and its commander, Commander Salvador, was the winner in 37 air fights, and he is a survivor of the García Morato's Squadron."

"Once again, these men confront the soviets, against whom they bravely played their lives in defense of freedom and culture in Europe, and continue the glorious tradition of the García Morato's Squadron. Good luck, say your motto, and good luck we wish you, once again. "

The courageous behavior of the Spaniards allowed them to receive many decorations. Commander Salas received the German Cross (after receiving the 2nd and 1st Class Iron Cross), Major Muñoz, Captains Allende and García López-Rengel, and Lieutenants Lacour, Ibarreche and Busquets received the 2nd and 1st Class Iron Cross. The 2nd Class Iron Cross was received by the pilots O'Connor, García, Kindelán and Mendoza; the mechanics Urtasun and Méndez and Corporal Álvarez also received it. The rest of the members of the 1st Blue Squadron were decorated with the Military Merit Cross with Swords.

2nd Squadron

The 2nd Expeditionary Squadron should have had Commander Muñoz, who had died in Russia when flying with the 1st Squadron, as its leader. It was necessary to choose a new chief: Commander Julio Salvador Díaz-Benjumea. He was a great prestige officer and had achieved 23 air victories and a downed balloon during the SCW (he was the only survivor of the famous Blue Patrol that fought in the Spanish skies). The position he was in before being assigned to the 2nd Blue Squadron was head of the Fighter School in Reus, so everything he learned in the Russian skies could be used to train the new Spanish pilots. The new squadron leader would be officially named "inspector commander", as it will happen in the 3rd, 4th and 5th Squadrons. This appointment allowed the direct command of the squadron in combat fell on the oldest captain, the commander inspector may perform other tasks than flying in combat (administrative, diplomatic and above all learning everything that could be useful for implement it in the Spanish EdA operability, etc.)

The Squadron was formed on February 6, 1942 in Morón (in Seville) where they had a training period until March 2 (the Tablada base was also used near Seville to which they arrived on February 8). During the training the pilots flew in the Messerschmidt Bf 109 B (bipala or two bladed propeller) and Bf 109 E (tripala) to get familiarized with the aircraft they would use in Russia, although Cr.32 and the

Bücker Jüngmann were also used. In this Squadron, unlike the 1st Squadron, the pilots came from three different situations:

- Young pilots aged 19-20 who had just received their pilot degrees at the Fighter School.

- Veteran SCW pilots.

- Officers who had participated in the SCW but not as pilots but in other branches (cavalry, infantry, etc.) and who had completed the pilot course after completing the war in Spain.

There were many requests to enter the Squadron, but eventually there would be only 15 pilots chosen, along with the commander inspector and his second boss.

On February 24, the Squadron departed for the Getafe air base (Madrid). On February 28, the 2nd Blue Squadron departed for Berlin as did the members of the 1st Squadron (who they had to pass by when they returned to Madrid). On March 1, they stopped in San Sebastian and later went to France, where upon arrival in Hendaye, apart from the welcome, they had to undergo the pertinent medical examination, as happened with the 1st Squadron. The trip continued without further delay passing through Bordeaux, Paris and Frankfurt, arriving at Werneuchen on March 4 at 9.30 am, where after being distributed and accommodated, the 2nd Squadron began its instruction the following day. But the initial instruction was not with the aircraft but completely theoretical (Eastern Front war situation, cartography, armament, how to make emergency landings in Russia, silhouettes of Soviet aircraft, etc.) what made the Spanish pilots impatient. The situation on the Eastern Front was favorable to Germany and after what happened with the 1st Blue Squadron, they were taking a long time to adequately train the pilots of the 2nd Squadron. On March 17, the Spaniards oath to the flag using the German uniform for the first time, since until then they had only used the Spanish uniform (the uniform was the same used by the Germans but in the right upper sleeve there was the shield-like national emblem in red/yellow/red with a black outline and the word SPAIN on the top), with the presence of General Gallarza, visiting Germany with the purpose of obtaining new German aid for the Spanish aeronautical industry as the construction under patent of Bf 109 or He 111. The feeling of the Spanish officers was that they were being treated as recruits and not as what they really were, but the strict German organization did not allow for a different way for the Squadron organization.

The Spanish pilots could finally fly on March 23 with 2 Bf 109 E, which were not the same aircraft model that would receive the 2nd Squadron: the Messerschmidt Bf 109 F2 (on April 25 the Spaniards received with great joy and expectation the news that they would fly in the Model F, although they could not do it until the second week in May). The time they had to stay in Werneuchen lasted until the beginning of June because of the delay of the Luftwaffe giving them their 15 Bf 109 F (these were planes that had been used by other units of the Luftwaffe and required a start point before being delivered to the Spanish). This delay allowed the Spanish pilots to successfully complete their training period.

On May 28, the entire squadron flew for the first time. During the long training period, there were several mechanical problems with the aircraft that led to several emergency landings.

On June 4, a simulation of a Ju 87 flight formation escort was carried out, with great success by the Spanish pilots. On June 8, the 2nd Squadron training finished. Finally, once their airplanes were ready, on June 17 (after about 4 months of training) the Squadron arrived at its operational base at the Orel-west aerodrome (about 360 kilometers southwest of Moscow) after a flight with several stops that caused the temporary casualty or the delay of three pilots (the ground echelon departed from Werneuchen on the 15th). To reach Orel there were several stops that both the Spanish Bf 109 and the Ju 52 had to do: Colber, Elbig, Königsberg, Neukuhren, Vilna, Bobruisk and finally Orel. From this aerodrome the Squadron began operating from June 21, which was the day that the Spaniards arrived at their new base. The destination unit of the 2nd Squadron was not JG 27 as it was with the 1st Squadron but it was JG 51 instead; being called 15.(span.)/JG 51. The Spanische Jagdstaffel (as the Squadron was colloquially called in German) was operationally assigned to II.Gruppe and was deployed in the join area of the Army Group Center southern flank and the Army Group South northern flank. Operationally the JG 51 and therefore the Blue Squadron depended on the Luftwaffenkommando Ost. Although it was only a Squadron, this reinforcement was very well received by its JG 51 German comrades. The Spanish pilots were also very satisfied to belong to the JG 51 since this represented that they would be employed in Fighter tasks and not in ground attack as it happened to the 1st Blue Squadron.

We have commented that the Spanish Bf 109 F were accompanied by a Spanish Ju 52 with Spanish pilots wearing the Luftwaffe uniform and the aircraft with Luftwaffe badges. This is due to the fact that the Squadron was assigned a Junkers Ju 52/3m aircraft whose owner was the Spanish airline Iberia, which made the route Berlin-Blue Squadron-Blue Division acting as both liaison and mail plane for the two Spanish expeditionary units in Russia (in fact the pilot of the plane was Lieutenant Menéndez) since one was in the north sector and the other in the center sector. With the help of this Ju 52 the transfer of the Spaniards to Orel was much more comfortable.

The 2nd Expeditionary Squadron had 19 pilot officers, 2 mechanic officers, 20 mechanics, 2 armorers officers, 10 armorers, 1 non-commissioned officer and 5 radio soldiers, 1 medical captain, 1 ensign chaplain, 1 intendance officer, 6 HQ non-commissioned officers, 9 driving and mechanical soldiers; 1 officer and 40 aviation troop soldiers. Therefore, the total was 1 chief, 18 pilots, 7 ground service officers, 8 non-commissioned officers and 85 soldiers; being the total of 119 men.

The 2nd Squadron was distributed as follows:

Stab: Chief: commander Salvador Díaz-Benjumea; Second boss: Captain Noriega.

1st Patrol: Captain Bengoechea, captain de Frutos, Lieutenant Escudé, Lieutenant Arango, Lieutenant Medrano and Ensign González Lafuente.

2nd Patrol: Captain Serra, Lieutenant Ripollés, Lieutenant Arraiza, Lieutenant Robles, Ensign Navarro and Ensign Beriain.

3rd Patrol: Lieutenant Barañano, Lieutenant Garret, Lieutenant Urquiola, Lieutenant Martínez Pérez-Galdós and Ensign Bengoa.

The 2nd Squadron also carried in the aircraft its own badge that was the emblem of the Morato´s Group (used already in the 1st Squadron) on a red cross of Saint James (Saint Jacques).

It was decided that a couple of planes should always be in Alarm status. These aircraft had to be ready for takeoff in a short time to be able to intervene in any situation of risk. The "alarms" were prepared from 3:00 a.m. until 7:30 p.m.

On June 26, the 2nd Squadron carried out their first mission, a Free Hunt patrol (the pilots were Commander Salvador and Lieutenant Garret). They found several LaGG-3 fighters (possibly 8) and bombers Il-2 (3) and SB-3 (4), but failed to shoot down any of them. The following days, they flew again in different missions without having their own losses or getting Soviet aircraft shot down.

On 27 June, the ground echelon arrived at Orel using trucks loaned by the Germans. The 2nd Squadron was complete.

Commander Salvador Díaz-Benjumea returned temporarily to Spain, where he remained until the beginning of August to contribute his knowledge in the war in the skies of Russia for the formation of the 3rd Blue Squadron.

When Germany began its summer offensive on June 28, the Army Group Center (where the Blue Squadron was) was not initially involved.

On July 1, the 2nd Squadron obtained its first aircraft shot down but also suffered its first loss: Captain Noriega. It happened during a Soviet attack on the Spanish airfield with Il-2s and LaGG-3s. Immediately, they tried to take off two planes (one with Captain Noriega and another with Lieutenant Robles). In the presence of the enemy, Robles could not take off, but Captain Noriega did and facing the superiority of the enemies, was shot down. Meanwhile they managed to take off 2 Spanish planes (Captain Frutos and Ensign Beriain) and they returned from an escort mission another 2 Bf 109 F (with Lieutenant Escudé and Ensign Bengoa). Already with 4 planes in combat, the Spaniards managed to defend the airfield and shot down a LaGG-3 (it was achieved by Captain Frutos with cannon and machine guns shots) and quite possibly another one, although it could not be confirmed (a LaGG-3 shot down by Lieutenant Escudé). After the combats, the 2nd Class Iron Cross was awarded by General Ritter von Greim to Captain Noriega and Captain Frutos. Captain Noriega would be remembered by his comrades when they painted the phrase "CAPITÁN NORIEGA ¡Presente!" (CAPTAIN NORIEGA! Here I am!) in the nose of Bf 109 F2 Black 1.

On July 5, another enemy plane was shot down when a Bf 109 F rotte (piloted by Captain Bengoechea and Lieutenant Ripollés) located an 8 DB-3 bombers flight formation. They dived over the bombers that were going low and Captain Bengoechea managed to shoot down one DB-3. On the same day, another pair of Spaniards Bf 109 F (piloted by Lieutenant Barañano and Ensign Lafuente) met another formation of Soviet bombers, managing to shoot down two of them (by Lieutenant Barañano). On July 5, there were other clashes in the Russian skies between Spaniards and Soviets, such as the Spanish aircraft pair (piloted by Lieutenant Garret and Lieutenant Urquiola) that faced a formation of 10 Soviet fighters, managing to shot down 1 Lagg-3 (by Lieutenant Garret). The 2nd Squadron also suffered the shot down of Ensign Escudé during the attack on a Pe-2 flight formation (the Spaniard achieved a possible Pe-2 shot down, but that could not be confirmed), but he managed to bail out and could finally be helped by German troops who took him to the Orel airbase.

On July 7, General Ritter von Greim imposed the 2nd Class Iron Cross on Captain Bengoechea, Lieutenant Barañano and Lieutenant Garret, for their brave combat against the Soviets.

Clashes with Soviet aircraft were very frequent, and that caused the number of Spanish victories to rise. The Spaniards missions could habitually be Freie Jagd or bomber, attack or reconnaissance escort. On July 11, after escorting a Ju 88s group, Lieutenant Beriaín had to make an emergency landing that ended up with the plane destroyed and the pilot with minor injuries. On July 18, 4 LaGG-3 were shot down without suffering the Spanish any losses. Two of the LaGG-3 were shot down by Captain Bengoechea and Lieutenant Arraiza during a mission in which they were escorting a German Fw 189 that the Soviet fighters tried to shoot down. In another mission, the pair formed by Lieutenant Arango and Ensign Navarro won the other two victories over LaGG-3 on July 18. While flying on a mission they located a LaGG-3 fighters flight formation. Immediately the brave Spanish pilots, in spite of the numerical inferiority, were launched to the attack and shot down 1 enemy airplane. Meanwhile another Lagg-3 was put to the tail of Lieutenant Arango's plane, but the quick action of his wingman Ensign Navarro managed to shoot down the Soviet plane and save Lieutenant Arango.

Unlike the 1st Blue Squadron that was very close to the battlefront line (and therefore had frequent clashes with Soviet aircraft), the 2nd Blue Squadron as the battlefront line changed, was more away from it each day, so the air meetings with the Soviets were decreasing during August (due to the German offensive against the city of Stalingrad).

On July 28, the mechanical corporal Tomás Zaro, in a fortuitous accident, crashed into the plane's propeller (already moving) and died immediately. As was the case with Captain Noriega, Corporal Zaro would be remembered by his comrades when they painted the phrase "CABO MECÁNICO ZARO ¡Presente!" (CORPORAL MECÁNICO ZARO Here I am!) in the nose of Bf 109 F2 Black 7.

After the month of July, the Squadron had 8 enemy planes shot down and 2 aircraft probable shot down in their tally. As a negative part, the losses in the Squadron began to increase and unfortunately it was not over.

On August 7, the Squadron suffered a new casualty. At 16.00, a Spanish aircraft rotte piloted by Ensign Navarro and Lieutenant Robles took off for an Fw 189 escort mission in the Mzensk sector. During the protection maneuvers to the Fw 189, Ensign Navarro clashed with his companion plane and fell into a spin to crash in the ground, losing his life.

On August 13 Lieutenants Urquiola and Escudé undertook an escort mission to Ju 87s. After completing the mission, already on the return trip they saw how some Soviet Il-2 aircraft were attacking a German vehicles column. Immediately the Spanish pilots threw themselves against the Soviet planes, while Lieutenant Escudé succeeded shooting down one of them after two passes. The others Il-2s were forced to retire due to the presence of the two Spaniards Bf 109s.

On August 14, the Bf 109 rotte with pilots Serra and Lafuente faced Soviet MiG-3 fighters, without any shot down aircraft. That same day the 20 services of war badges were imposed to the Spanish pilots who had obtained it.

Clashes with Soviet aircraft were not frequent, but on August 17 the pair (rotte in the Luftwaffe terminology) formed by Captain Frutos and his wingman Lieutenant Garret, spotted a DB-3 bombers formation, managing to reach one of them with the shots of their planes. The bomber was possibly shot down, but the Spaniards could not confirm it due to the response of the Soviet escort fighters that were launched against the Spaniards. Finally the two Spaniards managed to escape.

The next day the 2nd Squadron had the honor of receiving the visit of the German Fighter Inspector, Adolf Galland. Recall that Galland had been a member of the Legion Condor and had fought in the Spanish skies during the SCW.

On day 22, a formation of four Spanish Bf 109 (schwarm in German terminology) composed of Captain Bengoechea, Lieutenants Barañano and Atienza and Ensign Lafuente escorted a Ju 87 formation. During the mission they spotted 2 Il-2 flying at low altitude so Captain Bengoechea and Lieutenant Barañano launched against the Soviet aircraft. The Il-2 attacked by Barañano was damaged but managed to escape (although the lieutenant pursued him several kilometers, but the Soviet anti-aircraft artillery damaged his left wing and had to return), while the Il-2 attacked by Bengoechea ended up crashing into a forest due to Spanish shots. But after returning to the base, Captain Bengoechea participated on another mission at sunset on the same day after refueling (in this case his wingman was Lieutenant Arriaza), in which after attacking a formation of LaGG-3, they managed to damage and make land on an enemy plane. Bengoechea had become the Squadron´s Ace with 4 victories.

On August 28, the Spanish base suffered the most intense bombing up to that moment, carried out by at least 6 Il-2s (one was shot down by an aircraft of the German Squadron that shared an airfield with the Spaniards).

During September, the development of the fighting on the Eastern front caused the German offensive to reach the Don River and continue towards Stalingrad. As a result, the battlefront moved away from the 2nd Squadron air-base, decreasing the possibility of engaging in combat against the Soviets and thus to shoot down enemy aircraft in the following months. Meanwhile, in the Morón air base they had already begun to organize the 3rd Blue Squadron. In this case and unlike the transition between the 1st Squadron and the 2nd Squadron (which had been carried out improperly, causing that there were no Spanish pilots in the Luftwaffe for a few months), it was possible to overlap the march to Spain of the 2nd Squadron with the arrival of the 3rd Squadron. In this way it was thought that some pilots of the 3rd Squadron arrived in Russia before the departure of the 2nd Squadron and therefore sharing knowledge with their vet-eran comrades in the fight in the Russian skies. A group of non-commissioned officers and soldiers from the 3rd Squadron ground echelon left on September 17 to Werneuchen.

In October, the inspector commander Salvador returned to Orel after supervis-ing the formation of the 3rd Squadron in Spain. The group of non-commissioned officers and soldiers of the 3rd Squadron ground echelon also arrived in Orel. These men from the 3rd Squadron were added to the 2nd Squadron in order to get to know the procedures to be used on the Russian front.

On October 6, the monotony of the skies free of Russian planes finally broke as the pair formed by Lieutenant Escudé and Ensign Lafuente intercepted an Il-2 which they damaged but managed to escape (after the first burst, the arms of Lieutenant Escudé's plane stopped working). On October 9 before the approach of a Pe-2 to the Spanish airfield, the two planes that were in alarm status took off immediately. Their pilots were Captain Frutos and Ensign Mendoza, who managed to intercept the Soviet bomber and shoot it down. First it was Mendoza who fired and then Frutos, exploding the enemy plane. Although the days were passing without many clashes with the enemy, on October 13 the rotte formed by Lieutenants Barañano and Robles as they flew to fulfill their mission (which consisted of shooting down an enemy observation balloon) intercepted a formation of Il-2, managing to shot down one of them.

After these clashes, again the boredom seized the Spaniards who could not find rivals in the sky. The planes that were in alarm status were prepared from 5.45 am to 16.30 pm. Even the number of aircraft in alarm status increased from 2 to 4.

On October 23, the 3rd Blue Squadron 1st and 2nd Patrols left for France to be trained at the S. Jean d'Angely airbase (about 50 kilometers south of La Rochelle harbor). Meanwhile the 3rd Patrol in Spain was still forming.

The patrols that flew daily did not have encounters with Soviet planes in the following days, having to wait until October 29; this day Captain Serra and Lieutenant Medrano faced a LaGG-3 fighters flight formation during an escort mission to a Fw 189. During the air clash, Captain Serra managed to damage one of the enemies, although he could not confirm if it was shot down or not.

On the same day, October 29, the patrol that was in alarm status at the Spanish aerodrome (which was formed by Captain Bengoechea and Lieutenant Medrano) was ordered to take off immediately on the approach of a Soviet aircraft flight formation (7 Il-2s escorted by 5 LaGG-3s). When the Soviet pilots spotted the two Bf 109, the LaGG-3 attacked them. In the confrontation that followed, Captain Bengoechea managed to put one of the LaGG-3 in the target of his weapons, shooting it down (thus achieving his fifth and last victory, becoming the 2nd Squadron's main ace). While this clash took place, a second pair of Spanish Bf 109 took off to join the fight (Captain Serra and Lieutenant Pérez-Galdós) although one of the planes had to land again due to mechanical problems (Lieutenant Pérez-Galdós) so only Captain Serra continued flying. The LaGG-3 spotted him and it launched an attack against the Spanish trying to shoot it down. Fortunately for Captain Serra, he managed to take advantage of the LaGG-3 with his air maneuvers and to shoot down the Soviet aircraft.

October 29 had been very hard after many days without clashes with the Soviets, but no Spanish pilot was shot down and at least two Russian planes had been shot down.

During November, Germany began to have serious setbacks in different areas (Stalingrad, El Alamein, North Africa) that forced to transfer part of the fighters that were deployed in the USSR. Thus 4 Squadrons of the JG 51 were sent urgently to Tunisia at the beginning of November (Group II/51 and the I/513rd Squadron). So in the Eastern Front central area there were only two Groups: I/51 (with a squadron less) equipped with Fw 190 in the area of Vyazma and IV/51 in the area of Vitebsk (still equipped with Bf 109s).

On November 11, Lieutenants Pérez-Galdos and Medrano clashed again with a Soviet plane (a Pe-2) that was flying alone. It was easy for Lieutenant Medrano to position himself properly and then shoot the left engine of the Pe-2 and shot it down. This shot down aircraft was the last one that the 2nd Blue Squadron achieved in the Russian skies since their relay by the 3rd Blue Squadron was very close. The same November 11 took off to Spain the Ju 52, in which the ground troops Lieutenant Salvador Tomé was traveling, the first 2nd Squadron's man that was returning to Spain.

On November 18, the first 3rd Blue Squadron's men arrived at Orel after their training time in France. On November 30, the Inspector Commander of the 2nd Blue Squadron handed over the command to Ferrándiz, the 3rd Blue Squadron Inspector Commander, and the 2nd Squadron participation on the Russian Front concluded.

On December 2, the 2nd Blue Squadron first expedition under Captain Ripollés command left from Orel to Spain and on December 7 the 2nd Blue Squadron second expedition under Lieutenant Arango command did the same.

The 2nd Blue Squadron participated in 1312 flight missions, with 117 air combats in which they were able to shoot down 13 enemy aircraft. On the negative side, they had three casualties: 2 officials (Captain Noriega and Ensign Navarro) and a corporal (Zaro).

3rd Squadron

On September 1, 1942, the 3rd Squadron was formed under the command of Commander Carlos Ferrándiz Arjonilla (who was the only one of the Blue Squadron commanders who had no previous experience in air combat at the SCW). Its instruction began on September 17 in Tablada (Sevilla) and it was decided that the 1st Squadron veteran pilots would participate in the training with the ones of the 3rd Squadron while they were in Spain (Captain Ibarreche, and Lieutenants Lacour and Garcia got them started on the flight following the Luftwaffe training mode). In addition, all the training was supervised by the 2nd Squadron Inspector Commander, Julio Salvador. To facilitate the arrival of the 3rd Squadron, it was decided that men from it would join the 2nd Squadron in Orel (after spending only one training month in Werneuchen). Thanks to this organization, the 3rd Squadron's men would not suffer the various Russian front adaptation problems that the 1st Squadron had suffered.

In this 3rd Squadron, the Werneuchen airfield was not the one chosen to finish its training (except for the Squadron advance that was sent to Orel to collaborate with the 2nd Squadron), but on October 23 the 1st and 2nd Patrols departed towards the advanced Fighter training Saint Jean d'Angely airbase, (50 km south of La Rochelle) where they would be for approximately one month. In La Rochelle were the JGs Ausbilfdung Staffel (Training Squads) included in the Ergängzungs Jagdsgruppe Ost, which gave advanced training to the pilots arriving from the Fighter Schools. The training not only included the flight in the Messerschmitt Bf 109 F and G but also extended to other types of aircraft such as the Heinkel He 45 (old friend for the Spaniards), the Klemm Kl 35 the Arado Ar 96 or the Focke Wulf Fw 56.

The 3rd Expeditionary Squadron had 19 pilot officers, 5 support corps officers, 14 non-commissioned officers and 88 soldiers. The 3rd Squadron was distributed as follows:

Stab: Chief: Commander Carlos Ferrándiz Arjonilla.

1st Patrol: captains Asensi and Gavilán; Lieutenants Calleja, García Pérez and Roselló; Ensign Teixidor.

2nd Patrol: captains Alós and Hevia; lieutenants Luca de Tena, Azqueta Lacruz and Martínez.

3rd Patrol: captains Gracia and Ozores; Lieutenants Pérez and Meneses; alféreces Guibert and Aldecoa.

2nd Squadron Pilots who remained temporarily in service with the 3rd Squadron: lieutenants Beriain, Barañano, Bengoa, Garret, Martínez and Urquiola.

From all the Squadron´s pilots, only Lieutenant Luca de Tena had achieved an air victory in the SCW, but some other pilots had flown during the conflict in Spain, although not only fighters, but also attack aircraft or seaplanes (this is the case of Captain Hevia, who, coming from seaplanes, became a great fighter pilot).

After finish the training in France on November 11, 1942, the Squadron moved to Orel, where it began its active service on December 1. There they collected the planes used by the Spanish 2nd Squadron, along with some more Bf 109 F-4 (and F2). Also 6 pilots of the 2nd Squadron remained added to the 3rd Squadron (Barañano, Beriain, Bengoa, Garret, Martínez and Urquiola), since only 2/3 of their nominal number of pilots had been incorporated because the 3rd Squadron 3rd Patrol joined later. When all the 3rd Squadron pilots finally arrived at the front, the 2nd Squadron pilots were repatriated. It was on December 1 when the 3rd Patrol pilots began to join the rest of the 3rd Squadron men (although it was not until March 1943 that the unit was as full as it was when the 2nd Squadron pilots that were added to the 3rd Squadron returned to Spain).

The first flights that were made consisted of orientation and reconnaissance flights and were formed by two pilots (one from the 2nd Squadron and another one from the 3rd Squadron).

On December 1, the Squadron suffered its first casualty, Captain Asensi (who was the Squadron leader after Commander Ferrándiz). While carrying out a mission on enemy territory, the plane's engine failed and he had to make an emergency landing with the engine stopped. When landing very close to the enemy lines, he was captured by the Soviets (he was a prisoner of the Soviets for 10 years in which he led a Spanish POWs group that refused to succumb to Soviet pressure, returning to Spain on the ship Semiramis on April 2, 1954 together with the Spanish prisoners belonging to the Blue Division and the Waffen SS). After the loss of Captain Asensi, the command passed to Captain Alós.

The Spanish Squadron action area ran from Kirov to Liwny, being Mzensk the nearest area in the front. As happened to the 2nd Squadron, during December the main battles in the Russian front were in the area of Stalingrad, so that the air clashes with the Soviets were scarce. It was necessary to wait until December 27 for the 3rd Squadron to achieve its first victory. It happened during a Bf 109 rotte mission piloted by Lieutenants Lacruz and Barañano who spotted an Il-2. Lieutenant Lacruz threw himself at the Soviet plane, damaging it but receiving return shots from the Il-2. Lieutenant Barañano joined the attack and managed to shoot down the plane (Lacruz's cockpit was rendered useless by staining the oil that the Il-2 detached and had to interrupt the attack). The victory was achieved, but Lacruz's plane was damaged and had to make an emergency landing inside the German lines so he could return to his air base without problems. On the same day, Lieutenant Luca de Tena managed to shot down a Pe-2 he had intercepted during a mission. Thanks to the 2 victories achieved on December 27, the 3rd Squadron finished the year with 2 victories.

In January, with the fighting in Stalingrad coming to an end, the sightings of Soviet aircraft in the Orel area became more frequent. The weather was very hard with blizzards and temperatures that exceeded 30 degrees below zero.

The Orel area was heavily populated by Soviet guerrillas who made it difficult for the German rearguard units to carry out tasks and also affected the air units. In particular on New Year's Day of 1943 the Spanish Ju 52 piloted by Lieutenant Meléndez, who was carrying mails and packages, was damaged by shots fired by the guerrillas, while the plane was flying at low altitude for the Siverskaya aerodrome (near Leningrad) where the Blue Division was. The pilot's ability allowed him to land without significant damage on the plane despite having been shot in his left foot.

As in the previous squadrons, the existence of a couple of aircraft in an alarm status was maintained to react quickly to any approaching enemy. On January 12, Lieutenant Lacruz was sitting on his Bf 109 belonging to the pair of aircraft in an alarm status, when he received information that referred to Soviet aircraft approaching. Lieutenant Lacruz, due to the hurry, he tried to take off the Bf 109 before the engine had enough power to make them, so the plane crashed and Lacruz got seriously injured and had to be sent to Berlin. In a short time, the Squadron had lost 2 pilots and had only achieved 2 air victories, so the morale of the Squadron was not very high. It was necessary that they started achieving victories so that the dynamics of the Squadron improved; and it did not take long for this to happen.

January 27 was cold, as was usual every day since the Squadron arrived in Orel, but that day the luck changed in favor of the Spanish pilots. The couple formed by Lieutenant Barañano and Ensign Martínez spotted a two-engine Pe-2s formation. They launched the attack and on the first pass each pilot managed to shoot down one plane each. With the fleeing Soviet planes, Barañano and Martínez launched themselves on a plane each, managing to shoot down another 2 Pe-2s (the Pe-2 shot down by Barañano managed to land with little damage, but the Spaniard machine-gunned it once his crew had moved away). Four planes shot down in just a few minutes was a great success, but it was only the beginning of the day as the pair of Bf 109 piloted by Captain Hevia and Lieutenant Beriaín spotted several LaGG-3 fighters while escorting a Fw 189. They attacked the German reconnaissance plane so the two Spaniards reacted quickly and in the subsequent combat managed to shoot down two LaGG-3s. The remaining LaGG-3s persisted in their efforts to overthrow the Fw 189, but Beriaín managed to get in shooting position in front of one of them, and knocked him down. There had been 7 victories obtained by the Spaniards in a single day, which allowed the morale of the Squadron to rise after almost two months of combat missions that had already taken place.

On January 28, the rotte formed by Captain Alós and Lt. Calleja had a clash with 5 LaGG-3s while escorting He 111 bombers. In the subsequent combat there were no casualties, neither Spaniards, nor Germans, nor Soviets. The same day, a Spanish pilot (Lieutenant Roselló) was injured by having engine problems when landing that caused the plane to crash. Lieutenant Roselló had to be transferred to Poland for his recovery.

On January 30, Captain Gavilán carried out a Free Hunt mission with Lieutenant Pérez (who was the wingman). During the flight they located an I-153 that was flying at very low altitude and perfectly camouflaged to pass unnoticed in the Russian winter landscape. The two Spaniards had to get very close to the I-153 until they finally located it thanks to the red color of the stars on the wings. Once it was confirmed that it was a plane and that it was an enemy, Gavilan shot it and the aircraft was shot down.

During February, what was already suspected since January was confirmed: Russian planes reappeared in the Orel area. Evidently the German failure in Stalingrad was the spark that initiated the definitive change in the war effort on the Eastern Front. This situation motivated that the combat missions in which Spanish pilots flew also increased in number.

The weather was not favorable, and that led to several accidents like the one suffered by Lt. Calleja upon landing after escorting He 111 bombers. The plane was damaged but the pilot was unharmed.

On the 5th, Commander Ferrándiz and Captain Alós participated in a Ju 87s escort mission. During the mission they located 7 Il-2s to those who attacked, but the Soviet escort fighters prevented the shot down of any Il-2.

On the 9th, a Ju 88 bombers escort was carried out, as well as Free Hunt missions, but there were no clashes with the Soviets.

The Soviet troops were increasingly closer to Orel and the Soviet bombings on the Spanish air base were beginning to be frequent. The Soviets came to occupy Rjev and Vyazma, but were finally stopped by German troops. Despite this, the missions entrusted to the Spaniards continued to be carried out daily. On February 15, several Ju 87s were safely escorted in the Maloarkhangelsk and Kurut sectors.

Finally, on February 17, 5 of the 7 pilots belonging to the 3rd Patrol arrived at Orel (Captain Ozores, Lieutenants Pérez and Meneses and Alféreces Aldecoa and Guibert), reason why the last pilots belonging to the 2nd Squadron that had been temporarily added to the 3rd Squadron, departed by train towards Spain. For its part, the Spanish Air Ministry, always interested in getting German war material, received the suggestion of General Krahmer that if the Spaniards wanted to receive air material from Germany, deliveries should be presented as equipment for a new Air Squadron.

On the 19th the rotte formed by Captain Alós and Lieutenant Martinez, machine-gunned a Soviet troops formation of in the Pokrovskoe sector.

On February 22, Captain Hevia managed to shot down a LaGG-5 (initially the evolution of LaGG-3 with radial engine, which was later named La-5, although in our text we call it LaGG-5 the most accepted is La-5), while Lieutenant Pérez shot down an Il-2. The next day the Spanish pilots had another day with several victories over the Russians as they were shot down 3 Il-2s (one Captain Hevia, 1 Captain Gavilán and 1 Ensign Martínez).

On February 24, the last men of the 3rd Squadron who had not joined them yet arrived at Orel; specialists and ground personnel.

But the clashes against the Soviets continued and new victories were achieved. On the 24th several He 111s and Ju 87s escort missions were made, and during one of them, 6 enemy planes were shot down. The Spanish aircraft rotte piloted by Commander Ferrándiz and Lieutenant Azqueta spotted a 12 Pe-2s flight formation with LaGG-3 fighters escort; immediately the Spanish planes attacked the Pe-2s. The result was the shot down of 3 Pe-2s. Meanwhile Captain Hevia and Lieutenant Aldecoa, maneuvered their planes against the Soviet fighters, managing to shot down 3 LaGG-3s. The next two days the bad weather did not allow new flights.

The uncertainty provided by the Red Army advance (on March 3 occupied Rzhev and on March 12 Viazma), motivated the Spanish Squadron to receive the transfer order to the Seschtschinskaja airbase, located between Orel and Smolensk to support the German withdrawal in the Rzhev area more easily. The transfer was made at the beginning of March (the transfer order was received on March 1); the pilots on their planes and the specialists troops in the Ju 52. The new sector assigned to the Spaniards ranged from Spas-Demensk to Shisdra and Kirov; and as in Orel, the partisans abounded. The first things the pilots did were the usual flights to familiarize themselves with the area and the search for reference points for air navigation.

On March 7, the first victories of the Spaniards were obtained from their new airbase. Four Spanish aircraft (piloted by Commander Ferrándiz, Captain Gavilán, Lieutenant Azqueta and Lieutenant Pérez) carried out an He 111 bombers escort mission and Freie Jagd in the Shisdra area. Ferrándiz and his wingman Azqueta located several enemy fighters, getting Ferrándiz to shot down a fighter. For his part, Captain Gavilán and his wingman Pérez also attacked, and Gavilán managed to shot down another fighter. The plane that Gavilán shot down was damaged not only by cannon and machine gun fire but also because the propeller of Gavilán's plane destroyed the Russian plane tail (after jamming the cannon, Gavilan fired with the machine guns but came so close that he collided with the Soviet plane tail and later hit him with his Bf 109 propeller). Fortunately for the Squadron, the four pilots arrived safely at the Seschtschinskaja airbase (Gavilán´s plane, with significant damage, managed to make the return flight without further incident).

On March 8, several Squadron planes commanded by Commander Ferrándiz escorted a formation of Ju 87 in the Shisdra area. During the flight they spotted an 8 Il-2s flight formation in low flight. Commander Ferrándiz managed to shoot down an Il.2. On March 9, Lt. Calleja shot down a LaGG-5 and Captain Alós shot down another LaGG-5.

The Spanish pilots were achieving more victories day by day, but always following the rules of chivalry. For example, on March 10 the couple formed by Lieutenant Garcia and Ensign Teixidor managed to land an Il-2 with great damage. The orders received by the Luftwaffe pilots was that if it managed to land, the shot down enemy plane had to be destroyed so that it could not be repaired and used again against the Germans. So the Spanish Bf 109s rotte saw that the Russian pilot was alive and that he was trying to escape from the plane when they were going to destroy the plane on land. The Spaniards waited for the pilot to escape and immediately strafed the plane in a couple of passes. When the two Spaniards left, they could see the Russian pilot who was firing them in a firm position with his arm raised.

On March 13, the Squadron achieved three new victories (3 LaGG-3s) thanks to Captain Hevia and Lieutenants Pérez and Rosélló. It was captain Hevia's sixth victory.

Ensign Teixidor, during a mission carried out on March 14, had to make a forced landing due to an engine failure in the Bf 109 he was piloting. Fortunately it was located by a German patrol (dedicated to antipartisan tasks) and managed to return to the Seschtschinskaja base after traveling 30 kilometers in two days using a sled and a truck. On the same day, more than 30 Russian Db-3s and Tb-3s bombed the Spanish airfield, causing one death and several injuries. A new bombing took place on March 16, damaging several Spanish aircraft.

The number of Soviet aircraft flying in the area where the Spaniards were had increased greatly and posed a great risk to the air base. This would be confirmed when the Seschtschinskaja base was intensely bombed by Soviet aircraft causing great destruction and causing a new casualty: a Spanish soldier (soldier Jiménez) was hit by shrapnel. The planes that the Spaniards piloted were very used (remember that some Bf 109s had been delivered by the 2nd Squadron´s pilots to the 3rd Squadron´s pilots) requiring a continuous maintenance to keep them in flight, and some others had been destroyed by the Soviet attacks. In addition, the Soviet bombing had caused damage in the airplanes parked in Seschtschinskaja airbase, reason why it was urgent to obtain new airplanes for the Spaniards and the chosen airplane was the Fw 190 A2 and A3.

The Fw 190 was a superb aircraft but the Spanish pilots had not received any training for it. Recall that the instruction received by the pilots was to pilot the Bf 109 (but Spain did not have the Fw 190 in the EdA). The possibility of re-instructing all the Squadron with the new plane or sending a Spanish pilot with several mechanics to Smolensk was raised so that they could learn everything necessary to fly and keep the plane in operation. This second option was chosen so at the end of March Captain Hevia together with a group of 3rd Squadron mechanics went to Smolensk to learn about their next plane, the Fw 190 (specifically the aircraft that was found in Smolensk was the FW 190 A3). Captain Hevia was not chosen at random but for two important reasons: he was a great pilot and this was demonstrated by his air victories and he also spoke German.

It is not the purpose of the text to consider Bf 109 superior to Fw 190 or vice versa, but what is certain is that both were aircraft with many structural differences and in the way of being piloted. The important thing is that the new plane that received the 3rd Squadron pilots allowed continuing with the Spanish victories in the Russian skies.

On March 18, the Squadron lost one of its pilot officers, Lieutenant García. He was testing in flight with a Bf 109 just out of the workshop when the tailplane broke and crashed. The brave pilot died immediately. On the 21st, Captain García was shot down while escorting a formation of He 111 German bombers. A formation of LaGG-5 fighters was the cause of the Spanish aircraft shot down.

March ended and the Spaniards' performance turned out to be very good since they had shot down many enemy planes, but the number of casualties in the Squadron was increasing. The Spanish pilots idea was that not all the Russian pilots were experts but there were many occasions in which they behaved like novices, facilitating the Spaniards work. But after the last casualties and with few Bf 109s in service, the Squadron could perform few missions while waiting for the arrival of the Fw 190.

The arrival of the first Fw 190 at the Seschtschinskaja airbase could have become a disaster when a German pilot confused the plane piloted by Captain Hevia with a Soviet aircraft. Fortunately the German missed his shots against the Spanish plane. Everything ended with some apologies from the German pilot towards the Spanish when both returned to the airbase.

While the 3rd Squadron expected to receive the Fw 190 and begin their training, it was decided that Captain Hevia (who had already learned the piloting of the Fw 190) in the meantime would be added to a German squadron that already used the Fw 190. On April 14 Captain Hevia was flying a Freie Jagd mission with the Germans when they spotted several enemy planes. The Spanish pilot managed to shot down a Pe-2 and a few minutes later he shot down a Yak-1: the first Spanish victories with the new aircraft.

The 190 Fw began arriving at the Seschtschinskaja airbase on April 22. As they were receiving the new planes, the Spanish pilots were learning their piloting and in just three days they were considered ready to go back to combat. Thanks to the Fw 190 powerful armament and the expert piloting of the Spanish pilots, many victories against the Soviets came soon.

On April 27, the Spanish pilots were distributed in two aerodromes: the first one in Smolensk (a group commanded by Captain Hevia) and the second one in Seschtschinskaja (a group commanded by Captain Gavilán), to obtain a greater performance of Spanish aircraft thanks to the use of the new "Freya" radar system. Again Hevia, thanks to the fact that he spoke German, was chosen as the person for direct contact with the German early warning system. On May 11, a JG 54 squadron relieved the Spanish group in Smolensk and rejoined the entire Squadron in Seschtschinskaja.

The Spaniards were learning many things while flying in the Luftwaffe: ways to fly, to fight, to take care of the plane in extreme climates, etc. But now they were going to fly coordinated by the radar "Freya" and as it was later proved, quite successfully.

The couple, who were waiting seated inside their planes in Alarm Status, were Lieutenant Pérez and Ensign Teixidor. The news came from the "Freya" and confirmed the existence of a probable air attack on the Spanish airbase. Immediately the two Spanish planes took off and when the Soviet LaGG-3s arrived they were already waiting for them at a higher altitude. So the Spaniards launched their aircraft against the Soviets and Lieutenant Pérez managed to shoot down an enemy plane (a LaGG-3).

The Spanish Government decided to send Germany a second Ju 52, to reinforce the liaison missions Berlin-Blue Squadron-Blue Division. So it represented an important improvement for facilitating communications between Spain and the Spanish expeditionary troops in the USSR.

On May 5, the Squadron lost another pilot, Lieutenant Roselló. A succession of failures caused the death of the pilot, since first the airplane engine failed so the pilot bailed out, but the parachute did not open and he crashed to the ground.

On May 6, a Soviet aircraft large formation (20 Il-2, 6 LaGG-3, 14 LaGG-5 and 45 Pe-2) was located by the "Freya" towards the Seschtschinskaja airbase. Not only the Spaniards "lived" on this airbase, but also German Fighter and Bomber Units (the latter was one of the reasons that had made the air base a main objective of Soviet aviation). The German and Spanish pilots took off immediately to face the Soviets. In the following minutes there were many combats that took place in the air. Lieutenant Pérez shot down a Pe-2, Lieutenant Azqueta shot down an Il-2, Ensign Teixidor shot down a LaGG-3 and Captain Gavilán shot down a Pe-2 and a LaGG-3. There were in total 5 enemy aircraft shot down without losses in the Spanish Squadron.

There was little time left for service for the 3rd Squadron´s pilots but they continued to achieve new victories. On the 7th, two victories were won (one Il-2 by Lieutenant Azqueta and one Il-2 by Captain Alós). Unfortunately another Spanish pilot, Lieutenant Pérez, was shot down by enemy fighters after having shot down a Soviet bomber.

In the second half of May, the commander Julio Salvador, 2nd Blue Squadron ex-Inspector and other Spanish pilots, transferred from France to Spain 15 Bf 109 F aircraft. But this fact will be reported later.

June was very positive for the Spaniards because despite suffering a casualty (Lieutenant Pérez González), 22 victories were achieved.

On June 6, the 4th Blue Squadron 1st Patrol arrived in Berlin. The change from one Squadron to the other began when the pilots of the 4th Blue Squadron first echelon (4th Blue Squadron 1st Patrol) were integrated into the 3rd Blue Squadron.

The Soviet attacks on the Spanish airfield were continuous and the damage was significant. During the attack in the early hours of June 8, a Spanish Fw 190 was destroyed. The same day, when a formation of enemy planes approached the Spanish airbase, the two pilots in "alarm status" took off (Captain Hevia and Lieutenant Pérez). After they intercepted the Soviets, Hevia managed to shot down two LaGG-3s; so Hevia's total victories were 10 at that time. Lieutenant Pérez managed to shot down a LaGG-5. More Spanish aircraft took off to clash against the Soviet planes, then Lieutenant Calleja shot down two aircraft (one LaGG-5 and one Pe-2) and Captain Gavilán shot down two others Soviet planes (one LaGG-3 and one Il-2); Lieutenant Azqueta shot down an Il-2. Another plane was shot down by Lt. Pérez Gonzalez in the same planes clash. Ten victories had been achieved but a LaGG-3 managed to shot Lieutenant Pérez González's plane and shot him down. This was the last 3rd Squadron´s casualty.

On June 10, a new massive Soviet attack on the Spanish airbase was devastating. About 70 Soviet aircraft were the rivals of the Blue Squadron and the Luftwaffe airplanes that shared the airfield. In the combats that followed, Lieutenant Pérez managed to shot down a LaGG-3, Lieutenant Meneses shot down a LaGG-3 and an Il-2; and Ensign Aldecoa shot down a LaGG-3 (although his plane was damaged by Il-2 shots and had to return to land). In the same battles, Captain Hevia shot down a Pe-2, Captain Gavilán shot down an Il-2, Lieutenant Azqueta shot down a LaGG-3 and Lieutenant Martínez a LaGG-3. Again, as happened two days before, 10 planes had been shot down, although in this case fortunately without casualties among the Spanish.

They had managed to stop the Soviet onslaught on the 10th in the morning, but the restless Russians attacked the airbase again at sunset with about 70 aircraft. This time, the exhausted Spanish and German pilots could do little and the airbase suffered significant damage.

After the two days in which 20 "Spaniards victories" were achieved, the 3rd Squadron first pilots began their way back to Spain (as it was commented, the pilots of the 4th Blue Squadron 1st Patrol had already arrived a few days before to relieve them).

On July 5, the 3rd Squadron ended their activities in Russia. The 4th Squadron took over officially representing the Spanish Aviation on the Eastern Front, with its base initially at the Seschtschinskaja aerodrome.

In the official 3rdBlue Squadron farewell, the JG 51 Kommodore Karl-Gottfried Nordmann discharged the Spanish with this speech (according to Neulen):

"Apart from the harshness of the war itself, with your iron will have overcome the cold winter of the winter, the dirt and mud of the spring, as web as the dust and heat of the summer. You have done your duty as only soldiers know how to do it, and the proof and reward for it are the magnificent successes of the Squadron."

The 3rd Squadron participated in 1,716 flight missions, carrying out 112 combats and shooting down 62 aircraft. The number of aircraft shot down was considerably higher than the previous two Squadrons because the number of Soviet aircraft in the area where the Spaniards were located increased a lot. On the downside, the Squadron lost 5 pilots.

4th Squadron

The 4th Blue Squadron was born on April 1, 1943 in the Alcalá de Henares Air base (Madrid), with the components of the 4th Squadron 1st Patrol. It was commanded by Commander Mariano Cuadra Medina, who was a SCW veteran although he had not achieved any air victory. In Alcalá de Henares they completed an instruction month aided by veteran personnel from previous squadrons using the Cr.32 biplanes and Bf 109 E. After 306 training flights, they were considered ready to depart by train to the Colomiers Air Base (next to Toulouse) where part of the pilots of the 4th Squadron 1st Patrol arrived on May 18. The choice of the Colomiers air base and not of the Saint Jean d'Angely air base was due to the fact that the latter did not have Fw 190 but Bf 109. They stayed at the Colomiers airfield for a month completing their instruction period trained by the Luftwaffe expert pilot Hauptmann Walter Stengel (from JG 51). The swearing of the flag took place on May 16 and was presided by the German ace Hermann Graf. The flight with the Fw 190 training period was approximately 7 hours per pilot, after which the 1st Patrol Spaniards were considered ready to replace their companions of the 3rd Squadron. So on June 6 they left for the front in a Ju 52, arriving on June 15 at their destination after making a stopover in Berlin.

The 4th Blue Squadron Stab and the 2nd Patrol finished their training in Alcalá de Henares on June 15, after carrying out 228 flights. Without further delay, and after preparing the men for the trip, on the 17th they departed by train for Toulouse. After moving to the Colomiers Air Base, on 18 June they began their training period, which was quite short since on July 4 they had arrived in flight with the Spanish Ju 52 at the Seschtschinskaja air base.

The aircraft used by the Spanish were the Fw 190 A2 and the Fw 190 A3, while at that time the Germans were already using more modern models such as the Fw 190 A4 and the Fw 190 A5.

As it had been verified with the previous Squadrons, it was very useful to improve the learning of the new pilots arrived at the front, who shared combat missions with pilots belonging to the previous Squadron, so 4 pilots of the 3rd Blue Squadron (Aldecoa, Meneses, Guibert and Ozores) were added until the arrival of the 4th Blue Squadron 3rd Patrol. The 3rd Blue Squadron pilots combat experience in Russia added to the 4th Blue Squadron was demonstrated with the 10 air victories achieved in the months of July and August. For example Aldecoa added to his only Soviet aircraft shot down along the 3rd Squadron, 6 more aircraft while it was added to the 4th Squadron.

They also tried to improve the Blue Squadron logistics matters, so a new Ju 52 joined the existing one to replace the previous one during the technical inspections and to better coordinate the Madrid-Berlin flights.

The 4th Squadron joined the front at a crucial moment of the war on the Eastern Front, on July 5, 1943, just at the start of Operation Zitadelle in the German summer offensive at Kursk. Like the 2nd and 3rd Squadrons, the 4th Squadron was incorporated by JG 51 in the VIII Fliegerkorps. The Luftwaffe had 5 squadrons in the front sector where the Spaniards were: the Blue Squadron, the I/JG 54, I/JG 51, II/JG 51 and III/JG 51 with a total of about 140 Fw 190 (from those that only 88 were in service).

The 4th Blue Squadron had Commander Cuadra and 19 pilots; and on the ground echelon it had 4 officers, 12 non-commissioned officers and 116 soldiers. The total men was 152, being the more numerous Squadron of which Spain sent to Russia. The 4th Squadron was distributed as follows:

Stab: Commander Cuadra.

1st Patrol: Captain Galarza, Lieutenant Lucas, Lieutenant Valiente, Lieutenant Sánchez-Arjona, Lieutenant Escalante, Ensign Mateos and Alferez Teixidor.

2nd Patrol: Captain Llaca, Lieutenant Sánchez, Lieutenant Lacalle, Lieutenant Vigueras, Lieutenant Arango, Ensign García, Ensign Chicharro.

3rd Patrol: Captain Borrás, Lieutenant Serrano, Lieutenant Cavanilles, Lieutenant Pareja, Ensign Estébanez, Ensign Recasens.

From all the pilots, only one had achieved air victories in the SCW, Lieutenant Serra with four planes shot down. And some other pilots had participated in air combats during the SCW: Captain Llaca, Lieutenant Vigueras, Lieutenant Lacalle and Lieutenant Arango.

The Spanish Squadron front received orders from its incorporation to the battle to be ready for a general alarm. The Spaniards began to fly in their Fw 190 on July

5, although only Commander Cuadra sighted two enemy planes but without any aircraft shot down.

With Operation Zitadelle already started, the Spaniards were immersed in a front zone with a great air activity, as it can be confirmed with the high number of victories that they would achieve against the Soviets. Despite the Spaniards' desire to be in continuous action, due to their "inexperienced" status at the front, the Spanish pilots were assigned to bases relatively far from the Kursk salient: a Patrol with 5 pilots was deployed in Briansk (the one closest to the Kursk salient from which they would operate between July 12 and 21), subsequently another Patrol was sent to Vitebsk and the third Patrol at its base in Seschtshinskaja. Due to the continuous need for Luftwaffe missions, orders were received from Freie Jagd missions to be carried out only by two planes, in order to perform as many missions as possible. At least two missions per day with about an hour and a half flying time were carried out with the different pilots. The days had many light hours, so the missions could start at 5:00 a.m. and end at 11:00 p.m., and moreover, the Soviet night attacks on the German bases, so that exhaustion would soon appear not only in the Spanish pilots but in their Luftwaffe comrades.

On July 6, the couple formed by Lieutenants Lucas and Lacalle carried out a Freie Jagd mission, although mechanical problems in Lieutenant Lacalle's aircraft forced him to make a forced landing resulting in damage to the plane and injury to the pilot (due to the injuries in the cervical region, could not fly more in the Squadron). At sunset on the same day, the couple formed by Captain Gavilán and Lieutenant Sánchez also suffered an incident while they were carrying out a Freie Jagd mission that ended up with the emergency landing of Lieutenant Sánchez inside the German lines.

Finally, on July 7, the 4th Squadron achieved its first enemy plane shot down. Lieutenant Lucas and Ensign Mateos made an escort mission for an Fw 189 at dusk. During the flight they located an 8-9 LaGG-5 formation (flight), and Ensign Mateos shot down one of them.

During the following days, the Spaniards continued carrying out Freie Jagd missions without further shot downs. Meanwhile on land, the Soviets on July 12 went from defending themselves to counterattack. On July 13, two Spanish planes "rottes" took off, one rotte was formed by Commander Cuadra and Ensign García while the other rotte was formed by Lieutenant Sánchez and Ensign Aldecoa. In their mission they spotted four LaGG-5s, Ensign Aldecoa managed to shot down one LaGG-5. On the afternoon of the same day, the rotte formed by Lieutenant Sánchez and Ensign García took off, joining the rotte formed by Commander Cuadra and Lieutenant Lucas who were already in flight. They quickly found 9 LaGG-3s and began the fighting in which Lieutenant Lucas shot down an enemy LaGG-3.

The Luftwaffe pilots exhaustion was very significant and the wear and tear suffered in the aircraft caused a decrease in the number of operational aircraft. In fact, on the 14th the Blue Squadron lost two pilots that were shot down. After receiving the alarm signal, two Spanish aircraft "rottes" took off: a rotte formed by Commander Cuadra and Ensign García, and another rotte formed by Lieutenant Sánchez and Ensign Aldecoa. They spotted a Soviet LaGGs flight and during the air clash, Commander Cuadra shot down an enemy plane and succeeded in shot down another LaGG, but Lieutenant Sánchez was shot down (although he managed to return to his base alive) and Ensign García treated to return to the base after having problems but they never heard about him again.

Also on July 14, the 4th Squadron last echelon left of Spain towards France. While the 4th Squadron was not completed, remember that personnel belonging to the 3rd Squadron were added to it.

The fighting was more frequent every day. On July 15, after facing several Soviet aircraft, (4 Il-2 and 5 LaGG-3), Lieutenant Lucas shot down a Lagg-3. Again Lieutenant Lucas managed to shoot down another plane (a LaGG-5) next day, to which must be added the plane shot down by Lieutenant Sánchez-Arjona (a LaGG-5).

After the German offensive first days, when it was necessary to send a 4th Squadron Patrol to Briansk, it was decided the return of the Spanish pilots to their base. On July 20, the pilots stationed in Briansk began to return step by step. But on the 22nd again a 4th Squadron Patrol with its ground crew under the command of Captain Llaca was sent to Vitebsk.

During the last 11 days of July, the Spaniards faced new clashes against the Soviets, achieving 2 more victories (11 victories and 2 pilots shot down in July).

August began with a German He 111 formation escort mission on August 1 at 3.15 am. Four Spanish aircraft piloted by Commander Cuadra, Captain Galarza, Lieutenant Arango and Ensign Mateos, took off to give protection to the bombers, which were soon located by Soviet fighters who tried to shoot them down. The Spaniards managed to shoot down a LaGG-3 (again Commander Cuadra). After returning to the airbase and having a short rest, at dusk again the Spanish aircraft had to give protection to a 60 He 111s formation. The pilots were almost the same as they had flown in the morning with the same mission (to which they were added in Lieutenant Sánchez). Again the Soviet fighters appeared and attacked the bombers, succeeding Lieutenant Sánchez to shoot down a LaGG-3, although it could never be confirmed.

If July had been intense in air combats, August began with even greater intensity. During the days August 3 to 8, multiple air clashes among Soviets and Spaniards, allowed to increase the number of planes shot down by the Spanish pilots. It was necessary to always keep the Spanish aircraft in flight, so all the Squadron´s pilots flew at least two daily missions (one and a quarter hours each). The urgent need for

Image of a Luftwaffe He 112 where we can appreciate the stylized lines of this plane. Only Romania and Spain used this aircraft in combat. [Public domain]

A Bf 109 F Nose belonging to the JG 51 in 1941. We can see the insignia of the Jagdgeschwader 51 "Mölders", an eagle head.

Close-up of the 1st Blue Squadron badge consisting of the emblem of the Joaquín García Morato Fighter Group accompanied by a Roman number two (II) in the nose of a Bf 109 E7 belonging to 15. (span.)/JG 27. [Courtesy of Asisbiz]

Adolf Galland, a veteran of the Legion Condor who fought at the SCW, visited (already as Inspector of the German Fighter) the 2nd Blue Squadron. The veteran pilots of the SCW, both Germans and Spaniards, continued to maintain a great camaraderie during WW2. [Bundesarchiv, Bild 101I-468-1421-35 Ketelhohn]

The Henschel Hs 123 attack aircraft (called Angelito by the Spanish pilots) was used during the SCW and in the early years of WW2. Captain Allende and Lieutenant Zorita (belonging to the 1st Blue Squadron) piloted a Hs 123 from a German Squadron belonging to the II (S) LG2 in support of the German troops in Dugvino. [Public domain]

The powerful Il-2 Sturmovik was a very difficult foe for the Spanish pilots in the Russian skies. 37 of these attack aircraft were shot down by Spanish pilots of the 2nd, 3rd and 4th Blue Squadrons. [Public domain]

Insignia of the Jagdgeschwader 51 "Mölders", an eagle head. Although the Spanish fighters belonged to this Jagdgeschwader, there is no picture where we can see this badge painted in Spanish fighter. [Free from Public Domain by Das steinerne Herz]

Six Ilyushin DB-3 bombers were shot down by Spanish pilots in the USSR; 5 the 1st Blue Squadron and 1 the 2nd Blue Squadron. This aircraft was completely obsolete from the first year of war. [Public domain]

Superb photograph of a Messerschmitt Bf 109 E3 belonging to the Jagdgeschwader 51 "Mölders" at Deutsches Museum München. The Spanish pilots who flew along Jagdgeschwader 51 used the F and G models. [Free from Public Domain by Arjun Sarup]

Nice photograph of a Messerschmitt Bf 109 F4 at the Canada Aviation Museum in Ottawa. This model of the Messerschmitt fighter was flown by the pilots of the 2nd Blue Squadron. The Ejército del Aire (Spanish Air Force) bought from Germany 15 Bf 109 F2/F4 fighters. [Free from Public Domain by Ahunt]

Magnificent photograph of a Hispano Aviation HA-132L Chirri (Fiat Cr.32) at the Museo de Aeronáutica y Astronáutica de Cuatro Vientos in Cuatro Vientos (Spain). 100 HA-132L were manufactured with license in Spain by Hispano-Suiza in Tablada (Seville). [By courtesy of Javier González AviationCorner.net]

One of the many planes that made forced landings in Spanish territory. The B-25D-10 of the USAAF did it in Melilla on January, 1943. The photograph shows a North American TB-25N Mitchell. [By courtesy of Pedro M. Moreno (AviationCorner.net)]

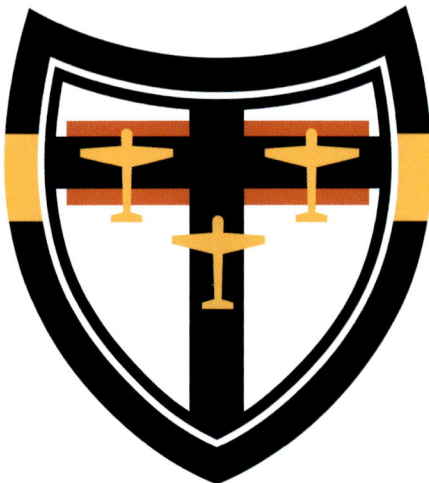

Insignia of the Jagdgeschwader 27 "Afrika". Only the 1st Blue Squadron belonged to this Jagdgeschwader, because the other Blue Squadrons belonged to the Jagdgeschwader 51. [Free from Public Domain by Shandris]

The image shows a CASA-Bücker 133C Jungmeister, which was manufactured with a license in Spain. Thanks to the arrival of this airplane and the Bücker Bü 131 and the Gotha Go 145, the Spanish aviation schools improved a lot. [By courtesy of John Mellor (AviationCorner.net)]

The Polikarpov I-15 Chato was an obsolete aircraft at the beginning of WW2, but the Spanish Air Force had many of them captured by the Republican side. Museo de Aeronáutica y Astronáutica de Cuatro Vientos in Cuatro Vientos (Spain). [By courtesy of Javier González (AviationCorner.net)]

The Consolidated Catalina PBY-5A interned in Spain on July 7, 1943 and later entered in service with Spanish badges, meant an important aid for the Dornier Do 24 in the rescue tasks. [By courtesy of Pedro M. Moreno (AviationCorner.net)]

In the photograph we see some of the Fieseler Fi 156 in the "Air Museum", which acquired Spain to Germany after the SCW. They were in service in the EdA until 1962. [Public domain]

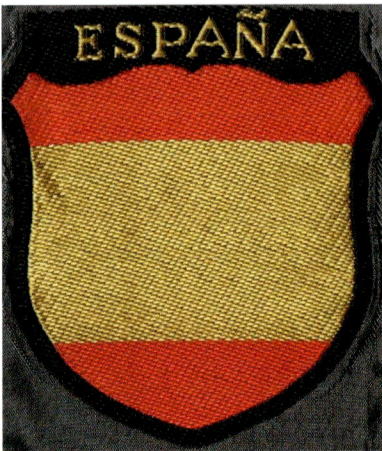

Shield used by the Blue Division, the Blue Legion and the Blue Squadrons in the right arm with red-yellow-red colors and the word Spain above.

Cover of the newspaper "ABC" informing of the return to Spain of the 1st Blue Squadron after "its heroic performance in Russia". In contrast to the 1st Blue Squadron, the last Blue Squadrons returned to Spain almost secretly. [By courtesy of Almena]

A German pilot gives a Spanish pilot some instructions about how to pilot a Ju 87 D. There were many missions of the Spanish pilots in which they had to escort the slow Stukas. [By courtesy of Almena]

Portrait of Ángel Salas Larrazabal, commander of the 1st Blue Squadron or 15. (span)/JG 27 according to the Luftwaffe. At the 16 + 1/3 air victories he achieved in the SCW, he added 6 more in the USSR (in addition to 2 aircraft destroyed in the ground). [By courtesy of Almena]

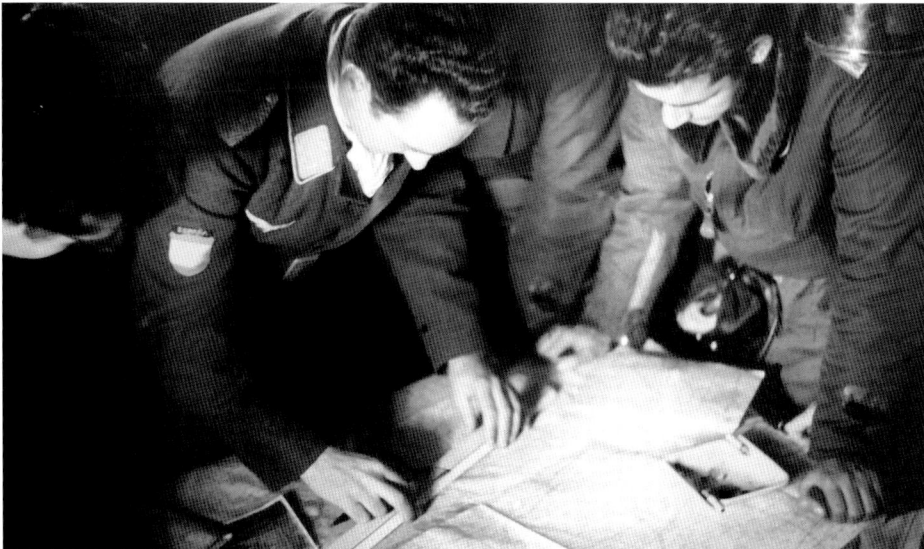

Several Spanish pilots in the briefing of a new mission in the skies of the USSR. It was very important to know all the details of each mission to fulfill it properly. [By courtesy of Almena (AHEA)]

A 2nd Blue Squadron Spanish lieutenant poses smiling sitting on the Messerschmitt Bf 109 F wheel, which waits along with several other aircraft, its moment to take off.
[By courtesy of Almena]

1st Blue Squadron officers pose for the photographer. Its pilots managed to shot down 10 Soviet aircraft and destroy 4 in ground. [By courtesy of Almena (AHEA)]

Messerschmitt Bf 109 E4 engine and armament photograph. The 2 Rheinmetall-Borsig MG-17 7.92 mm machine guns are clearly visible. This plane was very useful to the 1st Blue Squadron pilots both air combat and ground attack. [By courtesy of Almena]

A "romantic" photograph showing a 2nd Blue Squadron soldier guarding a Messerschmitt Bf 109 F. The 2nd Blue Squadron badge can be seen in the nose of the plane. On the helmet and on the right arm is the Spanish flag emblem. [By courtesy of Almena]

Several 1st Blue Squadron HQ members scan the "Pueblo" newspaper. For the Spaniards in the USSR, any information about the country represented a significant increase in morale. The 1st Blue Squadron badge is perfectly appreciated. [By courtesy of Almena (AHEA).

The Soviet fighter La-5 was a difficult rival for the Spanish pilots. 28 of these aircraft were shot down by Spanish pilots of the 3rd and 4th Squadrons Blue. [Public domain]

Julio Salvador Díaz-Benjumea, 2nd Blue Squadron commander talks with another Luftwaffe Squadron commander. It is clearly seen in the right sleeve the Spanish flag badge. His Squadron managed to shot down 19 enemy aircraft during their combat period in Russia.
[By courtesy of Almena]

Close-up of a 4th Blue Squadron Fw 190. This plane demonstrated its great potential when it was piloted by the 4th Blue Squadron Spaniards, who achieved 74 Soviet shot-down planes. [By courtesy of Almena (AHEA)]

Several Soviet fighters Polikarpov I-153 destroyed in an airstrip in the USSR. These aircraft, despite being completely obsolete, constituted a large part of the strength of Soviet fighters when "Operation Barbarossa" took place. In the small photo you can see the Soviet ace Hromov on his I-153. [By courtesy of Almena]

A Junkers Ju 52 belonging to Iberia (Spnish Airline) waits to take off. Some Iberia´s airplanes were transferred during the WW2 towards the Ejército del Aire. The Blue Squads disposed one Ju 52 (belonging to Iberia) with Luftwaffe´s camouflage and insignias. [Public domain]

Messerschmitt Bf 109 F2

Black 10 of 15.(span.)/JG 51, 2ⁿᵈ Escuadrilla Azul (Blue Squadron), Orel/USSR, July 1942. The aircraft carries the yellow theater band in the fuselage, yellow undercowling and yellow underside of the wing tips with black and white spinner. Teniente Arango López was the main ace of the 2ⁿᵈ Escuadrilla Azul thanks to the 7 Soviet aircraft that he shot down; the second ace was Capitán Bengoechea Menchaca that shot down 5 enemy aircraft (1 was probable).

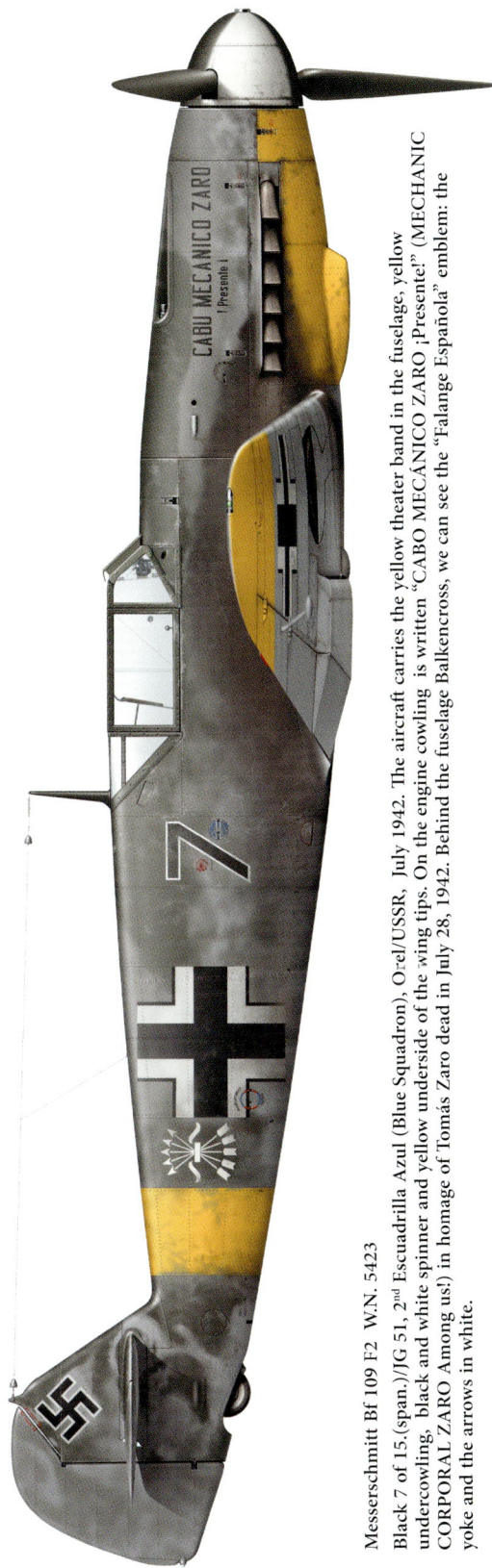

Messerschmitt Bf 109 F2   W.N. 5423

Black 7 of 15.(span.)/JG 51, 2ⁿᵈ Escuadrilla Azul (Blue Squadron), Orel/USSR, July 1942. The aircraft carries the yellow theater band in the fuselage, yellow undercowling, black and white spinner and yellow underside of the wing tips. On the engine cowling is written "CABO MECANICO ZARO ¡Presente!" (MECHANIC CORPORAL ZARO Among us!) in homage of Tomás Zaro dead in July 28, 1942. Behind the fuselage Balkencross, we can see the "Falange Española" emblem: the yoke and the arrows in white.

Painted by Arkadiusz Wróbel

Messerschmitt Bf 109 F2

Black 3 of 15.(span.)/JG 51, 2ⁿᵈ Escuadrilla Azul (Blue Squadron), Orel/USSR, Fall 1942. It carries the yellow theater band in the fuselage, yellow undercowling, black and white spinner and yellow underside of the wing tips. The 2ⁿᵈ Blue Squadron participated in 1312 flight missions, maintaining 117 air combats in which they were able to shoot down 13 enemy aircraft. On the negative side, they had three casualties: 2 officials (Captain Noriega and Ensign Navarro) and a corporal (Zaro).

Messerschmitt Bf 109 F2

Black 2 of 15.(span.)/JG 51, 2ⁿᵈ Escuadrilla Azul (Blue Squadron) in winter camouflage. Orel/USSR, Winter 1942. The aircraft carries almost full Eastern Front markings: yellow theater band in the fuselage, yellow undercowling and yellow underside of the wing tips but spinner is in winter camouflage. Behind the fuselage Balkencross, we can see the "Falange Española" emblem: the yoke and the arrows in white.

air support from the Wehrmacht and Waffen SS troops required in some cases that the German (and Spanish) fighters act on ground attack missions.

On August 3, Ensign Mateos shot down a LaGG-5, on August 5 Lieutenant Sánchez-Arjona and Lieutenant Escalante managed to shoot down a LaGG-5 each while flying as a rotte during a mission.

On August 5, the rotte formed by Lieutenant Sánchez-Arjona and Ensign Aldecoa (as wingman), escorted an Fw 189 and returned to the base, but they spotted 3 Soviet fighters (2 LaGG-5s and 1 LaGG-3). In the subsequent clash, Aldecoa managed to shoot down the 2 LaGG-5s (achieving at that time 5 victories).

On August 6, the aircraft rotte (Lieutenant Sánchez-Arjona and Ensign Aldecoa) took off from the Prost temporary aerodrome at 5.00 am to provide protection for a Luftwaffe´s Hs 126 reconnaissance aircraft. During the mission the Soviets appeared with 5 LaGG-5s and 7 LaGG-3s with the intention of shoot down the three Luftwaffe planes. The lieutenant managed to shoot down a LaGG-3, but he was damaged by the antiaircraft artillery fire which forced him to make a difficult emergency landing.

On the same day, August 6, another Spanish pilots rotte (Lieutenant Valiente and Ensign Guibert) while carrying out their protection mission to a He 111 flight, they managed to shot down 3 enemy planes (2 LaGG-5s were shot down by Lieutenant Valiente and 1 LaGG-5 Ensign Guibert).

On August 7, Lieutenant Meneses managed to reach the Ace category (5 wins) by shooting down a Pe-2. The next day, Lieutenant Arango shot down one LaGG-5 during his daily missions.

On August 10, the Spanish aircraft rotte piloted by the Ensigns Aldecoa and Guibert managed to shoot down one LaGG-3 each. During that same mission, the Lieutenant Sánchez-Arjona was shot down (saving his life, he was able to return to fly his plane a week later). On August 11, the rotte formed by Lieutenant Meneses and Lieutenant Sánchez, managed to shoot down 2 LaGG-3 (one shot down by Meneses and another shot down by Sánchez).

On August 12 they witnessed several Soviet aircraft shot down by the Blue Squadron. At 4.45 am, two Spanish aircraft rottes took off (one formed by Captain Ozores and Lieutenant Valiente and another formed by Lieutenant Sánchez and Ensign Aldecoa). Due to the attempted German counter-offensive against the Soviets in the Kharkov area, the support of the Luftwaffe bombers was necessary. On this occasion the four Spanish pilots escorted a He 111 flight on the Kirov sector. The Soviet fighters appeared quickly, and Lieutenant Valiente managed to shoot down a LaGG-5 with many difficulties due to the the Soviet pilot skill. Meanwhile Ensign Aldecoa managed to shoot down another LaGG-5. The LaGG-5 shot down by Lieutenant Sánchez must be added to these victories.

Only a couple of hours after taking off the first four Spanish aircraft, at 6.35 am, a new rotte piloted by Captain Llaca and Lieutenant Lucas who protected a Fw 189 reconnaissance aircraft took off. During the mission they had to face several LaGG-3s, getting Captain Llaca to shot down an enemy plane. That same day, two new Spanish rottes (Captain Galarza and Lieutenants Lucas, Vigueras and Escalante) were preparing to take off on a Freie Jagd mission. Because Captain Galarza punctured one of his wheels, he could not take off. The three Spanish aircraft continued with their mission and shortly after they found several Soviet aircraft attacking a German plane. They went to help the German aircraft, and in the subsequent combat, Lieutenant Escalante was shot down (he managed to save his life even though he was burned, so he could not fly again with the Squadron).

On the same August 12, Ju 52 (piloted by leutnants Calvo and Rego) arrived with the 7 pilots belonging to the 4th Blue Squadron 3rd Patrol of the. Finally, the pilots added to the 3rd Blue Squadron could return to Spain shortly. They took off towards Berlin on 22 August.

The next day there were no clashes with the Soviets, but on August 14, Captain Galarza shot down a LaGG-5. On August 16, Commander Cuadra was shot down by anti-aircraft artillery during a Freie Jagd mission, having to make an emergency landing at Katchinina. Fortunately, he was rescued by a Fi 156 airplane (where Lieutenant Arango was traveling).

Commander Cuadra, having been shot down on August 16, only had to wait two days to shot down a Soviet aircraft again. In this case, they were 2 (1 Il-2 and 1 LaGG-3). Also on August 18 another 2 Il-2 were shot down by Captain Llaca and Lieutenant Arango.

The combats during August were exhausting for the Spaniards, who barely had time to rest before starting a new mission. Apart from the "infinite" aircraft that the Soviets managed to put in flight, the Soviet antiaircraft artillery was becoming more powerful and dangerous every day. The losses among the Spaniards were going up and of course in their Luftwaffe´s comrades, the Kharkov front was resulting in a bloodletting in both pilots and planes.

On August 19 another Il-2 was shot down by Lieutenant Lucas while flying in a rotte with Ensign Recasens.

On August 21, Alférez Chicharro (who just arrived only 9 days before to Russia) was shot down. That day had taken off two "rottes" (Commander Cuadra and Alférez Chicharro, and the one formed by Captain Borrás and Lieutenant Arango) and flying over Spass-Demensk spotted several LaGG-3s, LaGG-5s and Yak 9s that they faced. In the battle, Ensign Chicharro was shot down, while Captain Galarza knocked down a LaGG-5 and Lieutenant Arango did the same with a LaGG-3.

Three days later, the Squadron achieved a new victory; in this case it was an Il-2 shot down by Lieutenant Sánchez.

The tasks of the Squadron's aircraft were repeated day after day, although sometimes different tasks were carried out, such as when on August 27 a Blue Squadron

Patrol (formed by 4 pilots and their planes) was sent to Smolensk. The pilots were Captain Borrás, Lieutenant Sánchez, Ensign Mateos and Ensign Estébanez. From the Smolensk airbase they carried out Ju 87s escort missions.

On August 28, the rotte formed by Commander Cuadra and Lieutenant Sánchez-Arjona during a Freie Jagd mission, managed to shoot down three enemy planes (2 LaGG-3s Commander Cuadra and 1 LaGG-3 Lieutenant Sánchez-Arjona). On the same day, on another mission, Lieutenant Arango shot down 1 Il-2 and subsequently Lieutenant Pareja shot down 1 Il-2. There were 5 victories in a single day, which demonstrated not only the Spanish pilot's skill but also the great facility to find Soviet aircraft in the area where the Blue Squadron planes flew. In the following days 2 more planes were shot down (one by Captain Llaca and another by Lieutenant Cavanilles), but on August 31 a Spanish pilot would be shot down again.

On August 31, the emergency situation on the combat front where the Spaniards flew led to orders from JG 51 indicating the need to carry out a lot of Freie Jagd and bomber escort missions. At dawn, the 1st Patrol (formed by Commander Cuadra, Lieutenant Sánchez-Arjona, Lieutenant Pareja and Lieutenant Valiente) took off to give escort to a He 111 formation. Soon after they were discovered by Soviet aircraft and the combat began. Commander Cuadra, with his usual courage, threw himself on a LaGG-3 that he shot down, although his plane was damaged and he had to make an emergency landing. Another Spanish Patrol (formed by Captain Borrás, Lieutenant Sánchez, Ensign Mateos and Ensign Estébanez) had to escort to a Ju 88 flight. They quickly found several Soviet fighters, out of which Ensign Mateos managed to shoot down one (a LaGG-3), but Captain Borrás was shot down.

On the same day, another LaGG-3 was shot down by a Spanish plane (piloted by Lieutenant Cavanilles). The Soviet pilots were not the inexperienced ones that faced the Germans in 1941. Now, thanks to the new airplanes models (Yak-9 and LaGG-5 among others) and to the experience of many of the pilots, they had become very competitive rivals, dangerous and difficult to shoot down.

During August, in the intense combats in the later known as Battle of Orel, the highest number of victories to date is achieved in a single month: 43 destroyed enemy aircraft.

September began just as August had ended: with multiple air clashes against Soviet aircraft. On September 1, Captain Llaca shot down 1 Il-2 and on September 5 Lieutenant Sánchez-Arjona shot down another Russian plane while flying as Major Cuadra's wingman. The fact that Commander Cuadra participated in most of the combats that the 4th Squadron held was warned by the Spanish Embassy in Berlin and transmitted to the Spanish Air Ministry (the idea that the squadron leader was at risk of being shot down was not accepted). Despite this, Commander Cuadra continued flying and achieving new victories. Other pilots who continued to increase their number of victories were Lieutenant Lucas and Lieutenant Sánchez-Arjona.

The Red Army continued advancing during September, leaving Briansk with great danger of being captured, reason why the Blue Squadron received in September 9 the order to move to Smolensk. The transfer was made as usual: the pilots in their planes, the specialist crew in Ju 52 and the ground echelon in trucks.

During the transfer, Lieutenant Sánchez-Arjona shot down a LaGG-5 (it was his 9th and last victory). From September 10, Spanish planes took off on their missions from the Smolensk airfield.

On September 12 Lieutenant Valiente shot down a Soviet observation balloon that directed the artillery fire.

Again the increase of Soviet aircraft in the area allowed the number of combats against the Spaniards (and therefore the air victories) to increase. On September 15, 8 Spanish aircraft commanded by Cuadra faced Soviet aircraft (4 Airacobras and 3 LaGG-5s) while carrying out a Ju 87s escort mission. The commander shot down 1 Airacobra and 1 LaGG-5. Another plane was shot down the same day by Lieutenant Arango (1 Il-2). On September 17, Lieutenant Sánchez shot down 2 Il-2, Lieutenant Valiente shot down 1 Il-2, Lieutenant Cavanilles shot down 1 LaGG-5, and Ensign Mateos shot down 1 Il-2. The Squadron was in the area where the fighting was more intense, which made them reach 70 victories that day (September 15).

But the situation became very complicated since on September 17 Briansk was captured by the Soviets and Smolensk was the next Russian aim. It is also important to appreciate that the VVS had not only increased the number of fighter that it had, but that the quality and performance of these planes was higher each day (LaGG-5, Airacobra, Yak-9) and their pilots were more expert. On the other hand the Spaniards flew with the powerful Fw 190 A3, but that had already been out of phase before the arrival of new models of the Fw 190 (like those that used their Luftwaffe´s comrades). Every day it was more difficult for the Spanish pilots to shoot down the Soviet planes.

On September 18 during an Hs 126 protection mission, the rotte formed by Captain Llaca and Ensign Estébanez spotted enemy aircraft. In the clash with the LaGG-3s, Lieutenant Estébanez was shot down and bailed out, but nobody ever heard about his fate again.

The clashes with the Yak-9 began to become more frequent, which meant a great difficulty for the Spaniards to shoot down them due to the excellent capabilities of this superb Russian aircraft. It is possible that some of the clashes of the Spanish pilots with the Yak-9 that took place those days, were against the Normandie-Niemen Squadron French pilots.

In September, the German lines had no choice but to retreat before the Soviet pushed so the Blue Squadron had to leave the Smolensk airbase on September 22. On September 25 Smolensk was captured by the Soviets. The Spanish planes were sent to the Orsha aerodrome to immediately be transfered to Stara-Bychow or Stra. Bychov (although eventually using the Orsha aerodrome).

Throughout this withdrawal period, there were no more Spanish victories despite having to fly missions continuously and the presence of numerous Soviet aircraft. Finally, the Soviet advance was stopped by the Germans in the Russian front Central zone in October, so there was a short period of time in which the Spanish pilots could rest after the maelstrom in the previous months. But the situation of the Axis was worsening on all fronts and the political and strategic situation of Spain definitely made it a possible target of the Allies. As we already mentioned in its corresponding chapter, Spain was forced by the pressure of the Allies to withdraw the Blue Division from Russia and of course the Blue Squadron would not take long to run the same fate (the presence of Spanish pilots in the Luftwaffe was not as widespread as the one of the soldiers of the Blue Division).

The battlefront finally stabilized in October, and the arrival of winter paralyzed the vast majority of air missions. The days went by with little activity on the part of the Spaniards, until October 21, when they faced Soviet planes again and Lieutenant Pareja was shot down. On October 29 Lieutenant Arango shot down an Il-2 and Lieutenant Cavanilles shot down another Il-2. The victories had returned to the Blue Squadron, which did not achieve any since September 15. But the number of victories would not increase much more, since during November none was achieved due to the departure of Spanish planes from the front line.

The cold, the snow and the ice caused the number of missions flown by the Spaniards to diminish, but in addition they were the cause of which the Commander Cuadra broke his leg after a slip (while it visited in Orsha a shot down Il-2 wrecks) and had to be evacuated to Berlin. Commander Galarza (who had been promoted a few days earlier) became the new commander of the Squadron.

The bad weather prevented flying for several days, but on October 19, a rotte took off formed by Lieutenant Lucas and Lieutenant Sánchez-Arjona despite the intense cold and ice. During the flight and due to an ice build-up on the wings of Sánchez-Arjona's aircraft, he lost control of the plane and crashed. He was one of the best pilots of the Squadron and his 9 victories prove it.

On October 25, the Squadron was ordered to move to the Bobruisk airfield (in Belarus), due to the Soviet advance. Despite the low visibility due to the fog, the Spanish planes managed to take off to go to their new base (at that time only 6 pilots were available). The rest of the Squadron personnel had to do it by trucks.

October ended with very few missions flown by the Spaniards and only with a couple of victories, but November was going to offer less possibilities of fighting the Spaniards (in only 5 occasions enemies were located but no shot down was achieved). The long distance from the front and the USSR winter prevented that the number of missions flown by the Spanish increased during December, although on December 5 Lieutenant Valiente managed to shoot down an American-made Douglas Boston. On December 11 Commander Cuadra returned after his hospitalized period, on the 14th he suffered a new accident (in this case with his plane) although he suffered only minor injuries.

During the following weeks in which the 4th Squadron was still flying, the number of missions was very small for several reasons: bad weather, long distance from the front and above all due to the small number of pilots who were still ready to fly (almost 50%). The time to be replaced by the 5th Blue Squadron 1st Patrol was approaching; the 5th Blue Squadron 1st Patrol had already finished its training period at the S. Jean d'Angely air base.

On January 9, the Spanish Ju 52 landed at the Bobruisk airfield, carrying the 5th Blue Squadron 1st Patrol (Captain Arroniz, Lieutenant Gil, Lieutenant Vega, Ensign Tassara and Ensign Orue). The relief of the 4th Squadron began to be a reality. Between January 19 and 22, 1944, the Spanish liaison Ju 52 made its last liaison mission, so it was no longer used to support the 5th Blue Squadron since the Spanish Government had already taken the decision to repatriate all the Spanish volunteers who fought in the USSR.

On January 10, the rotte piloted by Lucas and Lieutenant Cavanilles took off to protect a Ju 87s formation. In a few minutes they were detected by Soviet aviation, Lieutenant Cavanilles was shot down during air combat (approximately 5 German aircraft and 2 Spaniards protected 27 Ju 87s, who were attacked by numerous Soviet aircraft 5 times larger). Lieutenant Pepín Cavanilles was the last 4th Squadron's pilot that was shot down in Russia.

On January 12, there was the 4th Squadron pilot last victory; it was again achieved by Lieutenant Valiente when he shot down a Douglas Boston (A-20 "Havoc") from a 7 planes flight.

On January 14, the oberstleutnant Nordmann informed the Spanish pilots that they would shortly be flying in the Bf 109 G6, abandoning the Fw 190 that had allowed them to win so many victories.

The January cold days were passing by, not being able to take off the Spanish planes due to bad weather conditions. Moreover, the obvious air superiority of the Soviets made any mission a high-risk mission. In this sense, the Spanish pilots received the order not to fly with less than 4 aircraft in order to increase the protection.

On January 16, some pilots belonging to the 5th Squadron 1st Patrol began their flights accompanied by 4th Squadron veterans.

On January 24, the first Bf 109 G-6 arrived at the Blue Squadron. There were 5 airplanes that had been previously used by a Luftwaffe unit. On January 25, the 5th Squadron ground personnel arrived at the Spanish air base to work alongside the 4th Squadron.

On January 29, the 4th Squadron first men began to be repatriated to Spain. The arrival of these men to their nation went unnoticed since in those moments of the WW2 it was not convenient to give publicity to any men who had fought in the German side.

The Allies continued their pressure on the Francisco Franco´s Spanish Government to withdraw all Spanish soldiers on the Eastern Front. In January of 1944 the American ambassador Hayes asked for the first time explicitly the withdrawal of the Blue Squadron. On 18 February, the Spanish Government, through its Foreign Minister (Jordana), requested the German ambassador in Madrid to withdraw the Blue Legion (which was the small unit that replaced the Blue Division on the Eastern front) and the Blue Squadron. Only 2 days later, Adolf Hitler granted permission to the Spaniards to return to their homeland.

Despite the Spanish intention to repatriate all their soldiers, on February 19, a Ju 52 arrived at the Spanish air base with the 5th Blue Squadron 2nd Patrol and the Unit commander. A few days later, the ground echelon men began their journey to Spain.

On February 23, the 4th Blue Squadron officially ended its service in the front, retreating to Spain on February 28. The relief by the 5th Blue Squadron became effective on February 24, 1944 at the Bobruisk aerodrome, where the 1st and 2nd Patrols had already arrived (the 3rd would never reach the front).

The 4th Blue Squadron, whose ground echelon had arrived in Spain on March 22, was officially dissolved in Madrid.

The 4th Blue Squadron participated in 1918 combat missions, engaging 277 air fights and managing to shoot down 74 aircraft. When it was retired from the front in January 1944, it had lost 7 pilots (four officers dead and three missing), adding three serious injuries, which meant 50% casualties.

5th Squadron

The 5th Blue Squadron was created on October 26, 1943, in Alcalá de Henares (Madrid) following the pilots of the 1st Patrol a training period similar to that received by the pilots of the 4th Squadron, flying Cr.32 and Bf 109 E and trained by Spanish veterans who had fought in the Russian skies.

The training period for the pilots of the 1st Patrol ended on November 16. Due to the increasing political pressure of the Allies, on November 22 the 1st Patrol crossed the French border with special security measures in small groups and almost in secret to avoid attracting attention (there was fear that the French Resistance could carry out attacks against the Spanish). From the border in Hendaye (which the first men of the 1st Patrol crossed on November 22) they continued their train journey to the Saint Jean d'Angely airbase, where all the 1st Patrol men arrived on November 27. There, they did a one-month training period ran by the Luftwaffe using the Fw 190 (which was a small problem for the Spanish pilots and mechanics of the 5th Squadron who used the Bf 109 G-6 in their combat missions). On December 27, the 1st Patrol ended its training period with the "Ergänzungjagdgruppe Süd" (Replacement Fighter Group South) and on December 28 the 5th Squadron 1st Patrol men swore allegiance to Germany at the French air base. After a brief travel through Paris, the Spaniards left to what would be their airbase: Bobruisk.

But the 5th Blue Squadron was the last one sent from Spain to Russia, the one who would be the 6th Blue Squadron commander, if it was formed: Commander Miguel Guerrero, a SCW veteran.

The 5th Blue Squadron 2nd Patrol pilots departed by train from Madrid, crossing the border between Spain and France completely incognito in three men groups in order to avoid detection by the Allies espionage (in the past there were the reception with music bands and great parties as they happened to previous Squadrons). In this case, the base to which they were sent was not the one of Saint Jean d'Angely but the Bergerac base where they arrived on January 15. The training period lasted until February 6, 1944; only 22 days.

The training period in France was not very comfortable for the Spaniards, since the Allied air dominion caused the German bases to be attacked many times, making the suitable training of the Spaniards difficult. The relationship with the German instructors was good, as shown by the words of the flying instructor responsible for the training, Heinrich Heuser (according to Neulen): *"The training lasted until early February 1944. The pilots brought along with them good flying ability, high morale and a great operational willingness. During their stay with Ergänzungjagdgruppe Süd we also developed a good personal relationship between us".*

As we have said, the relief by the 5th Blue Squadron (only from the 1st and 2nd Patrols) was made effective on February 23, 1944 at the Bobruisk airfield. Like the 4th Blue Squadron, the 5th Blue Squadron belonged to JG 51.

The 5th complete Squadron had to have a boss, 19 pilots, 4 ground service officers, 11 non-commissioned officers and 96 soldiers; making a total of 131 men. This Squadron should be considered as the least experienced of all those who went to Russia, having participated in the SCW only 4 of the pilots. The 5th Squadron was distributed as follows:

Stab: Commander Murcia.

1st Patrol: Captain Arroniz, Lieutenant Gil, Lieutenant Vega, Lieutenant del Río, Lieutenant Seguro, Ensign Tassara and Ensign Orue.

2nd Patrol: Captain Carbón, Lieutenant Alonso, Lieutenant Sacanelles, Lieutenant Maura and Ensign Sanz.

3rd Patrol: Captain Díaz, Lieutenant García, Ensign Salto, Ensign Palanca, Ensign Cuadra and Ensign Gómez. This Patrol, as previously mentioned, never reached the battle front (as it happened to part of the 5th Squadron ground echelon).

On February 27 a Spanish Patrol took off, consisting of 4 Bf 109 G-6 aircraft (Major Murcia, Lieutenant Carretero as his wingman, Lieutenant Segurola and ensign Tassara as his wingman). The mission they had was to escort a Ju 87s flight over the Paritschi area. During the mission the two Spanish planes "rottes" lost contact and in the combat with Soviet planes, Lieutenant Segurola was shot down. He was the only 5th Blue Squadron pilot to be shot down (and also the last Spanish pilot of all the Blue Squadrons to be shot down in Russia).

A few days after, the 5th Squadron pilots could fly, without achieving enemy takedowns but also without suffering new casualties, since on March 15 the commander Murcia was called to go to Berlin (although the official order of repatriation already existed since March 6). There, he was informed that the withdrawal order for the Blue Squadron (and the Blue Legion) had been given immediately.

On March 18, the 5th Squadron (the 1st and 2nd Patrols) was ordered to deliver their Bf 109 G-6 aircraft. The 5th Blue Squadron official farewell was made by the 1st Fliegerdivision commander, Fuchs. The feeling was similar to what the Blue Division and the Blue Legion soldiers felt; they had been forced to abandon their German comrades when the war was becoming more difficult for the Axis. The Spaniards started to prepare all the material for their return to Spain, and on March 26, the Ju 52 with the 5th Blue Squadron pilots began their journey to Spain. The last men belonging to the ground echelon crossed the border between France and Spain on April 22. The 5th Squadron had almost one month of operative period within the Luftwaffe, so it barely had time to perform an adequate number of missions. Of course, the return to Spain was completely silenced by the Spanish Government, which did not want new problems with the Allies.

The pilots of the 5th Blue Squadron carried out 86 flight missions, participating in 6 fights and not crediting any shot down. They did not even join the full force, nor claimed shot downs, however they suffered the loss of a pilot (the shot down occurred when it was still the 4th Blue Squadron that flew in Russia but with pilots of the 5th Squadron added) and two Bf 109G-6, although one of them was not caused by the enemy.

CHAPTER IV

The Bomber Groups

As it happened with the other branches of the Spanish war aviation, after finishing the SCW, Spain had a large number of different types of bombers. These aircraft came from four great origins: the National Aviation, the Condor Legion (German), the Legionary Aviation (Italian) and the defeated Republican Aviation. The number of airplanes that were in flying conditions after the SCW was 84 Savoia S.79s, 42 Savoia S.81s and 10 Fiat Br.20s (these three types of aircraft were of Italian origin), 25 Ju 52s, 58 He 111s (22 type B and 36 type E) and 14 Henschel 123s (these last three types of aircraft were of German origin), and 18 Tupolev SB-2s „Katiuska" (of Soviet origin). Out of all these aircraft, only the Heinkel He 111s and the Savoia S.79s can be considered modern in the first year of WW2, the rest being obsolete (without taking into account the great wear and tear the aircraft had suffered during the SCW). This is the reason why many of these aircraft, although in flying conditions after the SCW, did not remain in the EdA.

As a first step we already commented that all the planes were gathered to later be deployed, following the Air Force new regional organization that was ordered by the Generalisimo Franco´s HQ on June 4. It entered into force on July 15, 1939 with the deployment of the bombers at their aerodromes. We have used the excellent work of González Serrano as the main source of information as well as various works by Arráez Cerda and the Historical Service of the Air Force and the Ministry of Defense on the study of the Air Force during the WW2 years.

The distribution of the bombing units was as follows:

- Center Air Region: at the Barajas airbase (near Madrid) with a Group of BR.20.

- Straight Air Region: at the Tablada airbase (near Seville) the 2nd Air Brigade was deployed with two Savoia S.79 Squads. The 61st Bomber Squadron, composed of the Henschel Hs 123 biplanes, also coexisted with them.

- Levante Air Region: with the strategic Squadron equipped with Tupolev SB-2 bombers.

- Pyrenees Air Region: at the Agoncillo airbase (near Logroño) the 3rd Air Brigade was deployed, equipped with two Heinkel He 111 Squads (one of night bombing and the other one of day bombing).

- Cantabrian Air Region: with the 1st Air Brigade equipped with two Squadrons (the 1st with Savoia S.81 and the 2nd night bombing with Junkers Ju 52).

It did not take long since the bombers were deployed to their airfields until they were deployed again at other aerodromes, shortly before the start of WW2. This is how the 11th Group was based on Barajas, the 11th (with the 12th and 13th Groups) and 12th (with the 14th and 15th Groups) Squadrons based on Tablada and Granada, the 13th Squadron (with the 16th and 17th Groups) with base in Los Llanos (Albacete), the 14th Squadron (with the 18th and 19th Groups) based in Zaragoza, the 15th Squadron (with the 110th and 111st Groups) based in Agoncillo (La Rioja), the 16th Squadron (with the Groups 112nd and 113rd based in León, the 17th Squadron (with the 114th and 115th Groups) in Villanubla (Valladolid), the 61st Squadron based in Tablada and the 11th Squadron based in the Canary Islands (still in formation). As of that moment, some Regiments (which as it was commented, replaced the Squadrons) were deployed in one or the other aerodrome according to the needs.

The bombers deployment at the beginning of 1940 following the text of José Luis González Serrano was as follows:

Regiment	Group	Aircraft	Number
-	11	BR.20	10
11	12	S.79	16
11	13	S.79	17
12	14	S.79	14
12	15	S.79	15
-	61ª Escuadrilla	Hs 123	12
13	16	SB-2	18
13	17	SB-2	
14	18	He 111	26
14	19	He 111	
15	110	He 111	13
15	111	He 111	13
16	112	S.81	9
16	113	S.81	6
17	114	Ju 52	11
			180 (136 in service)

From the beginning of WW2, bomber units and their deployment were slightly modified. Also the attrition and the wearing caused some airplane models to be used for secondary tasks like the Savoia S.81 that were assigned to the Aviation Academy during 1941, being the bomber deployment at the beginning of 1942 of the following way:

Regiment	Group	Aircraft	Number
Mixto nº 1	11	BR.20	10
11	12	S.79	27
11	13	S.79	
12	14	S.79	25
12	15	S.79	
-	61ª Escuadrilla	Hs 123	10
13	16	SB-2	16
13	17	SB-2	
14	18	He 111	19
14	19	He 111	
15	110	He 111	14
Mixto nº 3	113	He 111	12
			128 (90 in service)

As we can see, the total number of available bombers was decreasing progressively. But what was even worse than the previous was that the aircraft were older and completely obsolete compared to those flying through Europe at war.

This important problem was solved very lightly thanks to the acquisition of some copies of a modern aircraft type; we are talking about the German Junkers Ju 88. At the end of November 1943 it was possible to have 10 Ju 88 A-4 that were deposited in Albacete until February 1944. Also the EdA managed to have some more copies of Ju 88 (about 18 of various types, which will be discussed in annex I), thanks to the internment of these aircraft after finish their combat missions on Spanish lands and being requisitioned. The information on this matter is expanded in the interned aircraft annex.

In 1944 with the Ju 88s arrival, the bombers deployment was as follows:

Regiment	Group	Aircraft	Number
Mixto nº 1	11	BR.20	4
11	12	S.79	22
11	13	S.79	
12	14	S.79	25
12	15	S.79	
-	61ª Escuadrilla	Hs 123	9
13	16	SB-2	6
13	17	Ju 88	16
14	18	He 111	19
14	19	He 111	
15	110	He 111	14
Mixto nº 3	113	He 111	12
			127 (106 in service)

The bases where the different units were deployed during the final period of the WW2 were: Alcalá de Henares (Group 11), Tablada (Squadron 61st and Groups 12 and 13), Dávila and Armilla (Groups 14 and 15), Los Llanos (Groups 16 and 17), Valenzuela (Groups 18 and 19), Agoncillo (Group 110) and Son San Juan (Group 113).

Unlike what happened to the EdA Fighter branch, the bombers had few opportunities to participate in air strikes against aircraft of belligerent nations (remember the incidents with the S.79 in the Mediterranean).

CHAPTER V

Assault Aircraft Groups

During the SCW the assault aviation belonging to the National Aviation had achieved great successes against its enemies. The tactic called „chains" (cadenas in Spanish), in which one plane after another attacked a ground target with lethal success was within the history of aviation. After the war ended, these planes, like those of other branches of Spanish aviation, were grouped to be deployed starting in mid-1939. The planes that remained inside the assault units were the obsolete Heinkel He 51s and Polikarpov I-15s (a biplane from aircraft captured to the Republican side).

We have used the excellent work of González Serrano as the main source of information as well as various works by Arráez Cerda and the Historical Service of the Air Force and the Ministry of Defense on the study of the Air Force during the WW2 years.

The assault aviation deployment at the beginning of 1940 was as follows:

Regiment	Group	Aircraft	Number
31	31	He 51	44
31	32	He 51	
32	33	I-15	¿50?
32	34	I-15	
			Not known

Regiment 31 was based on the Getafe aerodrome (Madrid), while Regiment 32 was based on the La Rabasa aerodrome (Alicante).

There were no significant changes in the assault aviation deployment until in July 1941 when Regiment 33 (containing Groups 35 and 36) was created and it was equipped with the I-15 aircraft type. From this moment until the end of WW2, there were no significant changes in the structure of the Spanish assault aviation. As in the EdA other branches, the aircraft wearing and its fast obsolescence did occur. In the following chart, we show the deployment from 1942 to 1945:

Regiment	Group	Aircraft	Number
31	31	He 51	13-39
31	32	He 51	

32	33	I-15	26-44
32	34	I-15	
33	35	I-15	13-52
33	36	I-15	
			81-109 (58-82 in service)

Since these planes were limited in their action range and deployed geographically in central and eastern Spain, they did not intervene in clashes with belligerent planes during WW2.

Two planes belonging to the 4th Blue Squadron return to their airstrip making victory signs with their wings. The men of the ground staff greet them effusively.
[By courtesy of Almena (AHEA)]

Captain Hevia belonging to the 3rd Blue Squadron poses next to the tail of his Bf 109 F. There are five winning bars obtained by the Spanish pilot, who would finally achieve 12 victories. 12 were the greatest number of victories achieved by one of the Spanish pilots in the skies of the USSR. [By courtesy of Almena]

Captain Gavilán of the 3rd Blue Squadron poses satisfied next to his Bf 109 F showing his left wing shattered after the fighting on March 7, 1943. Captain Gavilán managed 9 Soviet shot-down planes. [By courtesy of Almena]

One of the Luftwaffe´s reconnaissance aircraft that should have been escorted in the Russian skies was the Junkers Ju 86 P, which could reach an altitude of up to 10000 meters. [By courtesy of Almena]

A Douglas A-20 Havoc (also known as Boston) with its Soviet crew. Three of these powerful planes were shot down by the pilots of the 4th Blue Squadron. [By courtesy of Almena]

Several Soviet fighters Polikarpov destroyed in an unknown airstrip. The Spanish pilots of the 1st Blue Squadron had to perform in addition to the fighter missions, ground attack missions. [By courtesy of Almena]

Another image of a Cr.32 fighter with the Spanish insignia on the fuselage and on the tail. When jet planes were already flying in the skies of Europe, the I-15bis and Cr.32 biplanes were still flying in Spain. [By courtesy of Almena]

A flight of Ju 87 D Stukas approaching their target. These slow and vulnerable aircrafts were protected a lot of times for the Spanish pilots. [By courtesy of Almena]

Visit of generaloberst Ritter von Greim to the 3rd Blue Squadron. In the photo you can see several of the 3rd Blue Squadron pilots, corresponding from left to right: Captain Alós, Captain Ozores, Captain Gavilán, Commander Ferrándiz, Generaloberst Ritter von Greim, Lieutenant Calleja, Lieutenant Pérez, Ensign Teixidor, Lieutenant Meneses and Captain Hevia.
[By courtesy of Almena]

The last Spanish unit officially fighting against the USSR was the Blue Legion (Spanish Legion of Volunteers), which coincided in time with the 4th and 5th Blue Squadrons. In the image we see the Spanish soldiers of the Blue Legion with German uniform and the Spanish flag flying in the air in Stablack-Süd. [Courtesy of Luis E. Togores]

A Focke Wulf Fw 200C Kondor with Spanish insignia, previously belonging to the Luftwaffe. This aircraft is the one that landed in Seville on January 1, 1943. The need for modern aircraft by Spain made it possible to make the most of the interned and injured planes in Spanish territory. [Courtesy of Rod's Warbirds]

At the end of the SCW, Spain had 14 Messerschmitt Bf 109 A and B. These aircraft were already obsolete at the beginning of WW2. The airplane in the photograph shows the typical insignia of the Legion Condor during the SCW. [Public domain]

Aerial view of the Tablada airbase in Seville in 1928. In this airbase, the 2nd and 3rd Blue Squadrons pilots were trained. Today it is still a military airbase of the Spanish Air Force. [Public domain]

On the left of the picture is Lieutenant Alcocer, who was the first casualty that the 1st Blue Squadron suffered when, on October 2, 1941, he became disoriented while running out of fuel and died trying to make an emergency landing. [By courtesy of Almena]

A Dewoitine D.520 from Vichy France. There were some air clashes among Spanish He-112 B aircraft belonging to 27 Group based in North Africa (in Nador) and Vichy France Dewoitine 520 aircrafts based in Port Lyautey (Morocco). [Courtesy of Rod's Warbirds]

Another Luftwaffe aircraft interned in Spain and later put into service in the Spanish Air Force was this Junkers Ju 290. This aircraft took years to get back on duty. [Courtesy of Rod's Warbirds]

A Fiat Br.20 belonging to the Italian 23 Squadriglia during the SCW. 13 copies of this venerable aircraft fought with the Legionary Aviation, of which 10 survived the SCW and were delivered to the EdA. [Courtesy of Rod's Warbirds]

In 1943 Germany sold to Spain 12 Heinkel He 114 seaplanes. These aircraft improved the Spanish Air Force rescue and maritime reconnaissance capacity in the sea. [Courtesy of Rod's Warbirds]

Several ground crew of the 1st Blue Squadron pose in front of a Messerschmitt Bf 109 E. In the nose of the plane you can see the 1st Blue Squadron. [badge Courtesy of Rod's Warbirds]

In the photograph we see a Fiat G.50 belonging to the Italian Legionary Aviation during the SCW. Several of these aircraft were acquired by the Air Force and were transferred to the 27 Group under the command of Commander Guerrero that was deployed in Nador along with the Heinkel He 112. [Public domain]

Photograph of a Legion Condor Heinkel He 112. Along with the Bf 109 E, the Heinkel He 112s, were the best Spanish fighters at that time so they were deployed all at the Nador airbase (Melilla). [Courtesy of Rod's Warbirds]

The Fiat G.50 fighters formed the 27th Group 2nd Squadron based in Nador (Melilla). In the picture we can see in this G.50 flying over Nador, the 2nd Squadron badge, a white greyhound jumping down inside a white circle. [Courtesy of Juan Arráez Cerdá]

Lieutenants Ángel Mendoza and Esteban Ibarreche of the 1st Squadron Azul pose for the photograph with a Bf 109 E, showing in their hands a handkerchief with the badge of the Fighter Group by Joaquín García Morato. [By courtesy of Almena (AHEA)]

Juan Vigón Suero-Díaz replaced Yagüe as Minister of Air, occupying the position until July 20, 1945. In the photograph as Lieutenant General. [Free from Public Domain by Jalón Ángel]

The arrival of the cargo ship "Semíramis" to Spain from the USSR on April 2, 1954 with the Spanish prisoners mainly from the Blue Division and the Waffen SS. Among the prisoners who were held the longest in the USSR were the Spaniards, and among them a pilot belonging to the 4th Blue Squadron: Captain Andres Asensi who was forced to take land by engine failure in enemy territory. [Courtesy of Luis E. Togores]

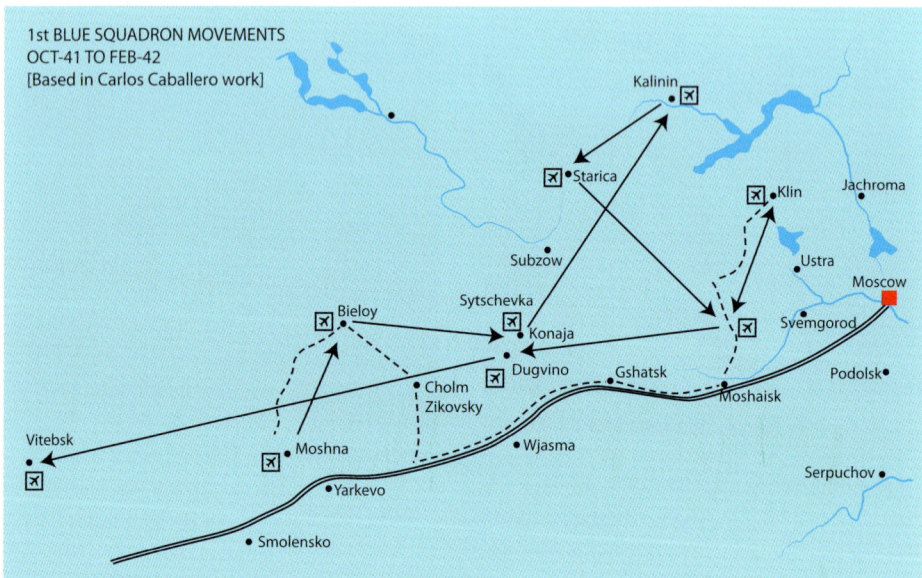

1st BLUE SQUADRON MOVEMENTS
OCT-41 TO FEB-42
[Based in Carlos Caballero work]

Kalinin

Starica

Klin   Jachroma

Subzow   Ustra
                                  Moscow
Sytschevka
Bieloy   Konaja   Svemgorod
      Dugvino   Gshatsk   Podolsk
Cholm   Moshaisk
Zikovsky
Vitebsk   Wjasma
      Moshna   Serpuchov
Yarkevo

Smolensko

Map with the main operational areas of the 5 Blue Squadrons

Kalinin

Klin

Stantza

Moscow

Rzhev

Volokolamsk

Bjeloj

Rusa

Konaja

Mozbaisk

Moschna

Vyasma

Vitebsk

Kaluga

Smolensk

Tula

Orsha

Bychow

Seschinskaya

Bobreuisk

Briansk

Orel

1st Blue Squadron operational area

2nd Blue Squadron operational area

3rd Blue Squadron operational area

4th Blue Squadron operational area
5th Blue Squadron operational area

Frontline 30, September, 1941

Frontline 15, November, 1941

Main German attack lines.

1st Blue Squadron Movement.

Places where 1st Blue Squadron was deployed.

Approximate location map of the interned aircraft that landed in Spain during WW2: Red: France (Armee de l'Air). Blue: Great Britain (RAF, RN). Gray: USA (USAAF). Green: Italy (Regia Aeronautica, Aeronautica Nazionale Republicana). Black: Germany (Luftwaffe)

Approximate location map of the belligerent planes crashed in Spain during WW2: Red: France (Armee de l'Air). Blue: Great Britain (RAF, RN). Gray: USA (USAAF).Green: Italy (Regia Aeronautica, Aeronautica Nazionale Republicana). Black: Germany (Luftwaffe).

Location map of Spanish aircrafts shot down by aircrafts belonging to the Allies and location map of Allied aircraft shot down by Spanish aircrafts during WW2: Red: Spanish planes shot down. Yellow: Allied aircraft shot down. Blue Circle: main meeting areas between Spanish and Allied aircraft. [All maps drawn by the author]

Painted by Arkadiusz Wróbel

Messerschmitt Bf 109 F2 W.N 9609

Black 1 of 15.(span.)/JG 51, 2nd Escuadrilla Azul, usually flown by Teniente Andrés Robles Cebrián, Orel/USSR, August 1942. The aircraft bears the 2nd Escuadrilla Azul emblem in the engine cowling, the same emblem of the 1st Escuadrilla Azul although on a red Santiago Cross (Saint Jacques Cross). It carries the yellow theater band in the fuselage, yellow undercowling, black and white spinner and yellow underside of the wing tips.Not visible (in the other side of the cowling) is written the sentence "CAPITÁN NORIEGA ¡Presente!" (CAPTAIN NORIEGA Among us!) in tribute to Captain Noriega died on July 1, 1942. Behind the fuselage Balkencross, we can see the "Falange Española" emblem: the yoke and the arrows in white.A close-up shows the "Falange Española" and the 2nd Escuadrilla Azul emblems.

Messerschmitt Bf 109 E4

Belonging to the 15.(span.)/JG27 or 1st Escuadrilla Azul (Blue Squadron). East Front. Fall 1941. The aircraft bears the 1st Blue Squadron emblem in the engine cowling and shows typical Eats Front German markings as the yellow theater band, cowling, spinner and lower wing tips. The 1st Blue Squadron carried out 422 combat missions, as bomber protection and Freie Jagd; ard participated in 94 aerial combats managing to shoot down 10 confirmed enemy airplanes, 4 probable and also destroyed 5 planes on the ground.

Painted by Arkadiusz Wróbel

Messerschmitt Bf 109 E4 W.N. 3297

Black M of 15.(span.)/JG27 or 1st Escuadrilla Azul (Blue Squadron), flown by Comandante Ángel Salas Larrazábal, Staritza/USSR, 3 November 1941. Comandante (Major) Larrazábal, the leader of the 1st Escuadrilla Azul shot down 6 Soviet aircraft and destroyed 2 in the ground. The aircraft bears the 1st Blue Squadron emblem in the engine cowling that was a white circle with three birds in the center (a hawk, a bustard and a blackbird) and the phrase "Vista, suerte, y al toro" that means "Sight, luck and to the bull" with a 2 in roman (II). The large black triangle outlined in white close to the fuselage cross was the marking of the Schlachtflieger (ground attack) units.

Messerschmitt Bf 109 E4/Trop

Belonging to the 15.(span.)/JG27 or 1st Escuadrilla Azul (Blue Squadron). East Front. Fall 1941. This aircraft was the only Bf 109 in tropical version that the 1st Escuadrilla Azul flew and shows typical Eats Front German markings. It carries the yellow theater band, yellow cowling, black spinner, yellow underside of the wing tips. The real name of the Blue Squadron was Expeditionary Squadron in Russia, but eveybody know it as Blue Squadron. Approximately after six months in combat the 1st Escuadrilla Azul returned to Spain, leaving in the USSR 5 pilots killed victims of the Soviet antiaircraft artillery or in accidents and a soldier.

CHAPTER VI

The Seaplanes Force

Spain used seaplanes since the 1920s, which along with the large number of kilometers of coastline and the possession of the Canary Islands and the Balearic Islands, allowed optimal use of them to obtain maximum performance.

After the SCW were several seaplanes models that had the EDA: from German origin mainly, such as Heinkel He 59, Heinkel He 60, Dornier Wal, Arado Ar 95 or from Italian origin as Cant Z.501 and Cant Z.506. To these aircraft they would be united in 1943 12 Heinkel He 114s and in 1944 the formidable and very valid Dornier Do 24. Several Italian origin seaplanes Romeo Ro.43 and Romeo Ro.44 were acquired by Spain to Italy (after their pilots looked for refuge in Spain after the Italian armistice of 1943) although they did not get into service before the end of WW2.

The use of these aircraft was a mixture of maritime reconnaissance and rescue (SAR) tasks. This task was carried out mainly in the Mediterranean Sea waters and to a lesser extent in the Canary Islands waters.

We have used the excellent work of González Serrano as the main source of information as well as various works by Arráez Cerda and the Historical Service of the Air Force and the Ministry of Defense on the study of the Air Force during the WW2 years.

The seaplanes deployment in January 1940 was as follows:

Group	Unit	Aircraft	Base
Grupo 51.	Escuadrilla 52	He 59 He 60	Pollensa (Baleares)
Grupo 51.	Escuadrilla 53	Cant Z.501 Cant Z.506	Pollensa (Baleares)
	Patrulla 51	Ar 95	Pollensa (Baleares)
	Escuadrilla 51	Dornier Wal	El Atalayón (Spanish Morocco)

There was a restructuring in the units, as well as after the arrival of the Heinkel He 114 in July 1943 the creation of a new Group to include them. Thus in January 1944 the deployment was as follows:

Group	Aircraft	Number	Base
51 Escuadrilla	Dornier Wal	6	El Atalayón (Spanish Morocco)
52 Escuadrilla	He 59 He 60	5	Pollensa (Baleares)
53 Escuadrilla	Cant Z.506	1	Pollensa (Baleares)
54 Escuadrilla	Dornier Wal	2	Puerto de Las Palmas (Gran Canaria)
52 Grupo	He 114	12	San Javier (Murcia)
		26 (21 in service)	

Finally, after the acquisition of 12 copies of the German-made seaplane Dornier Do 24 T-3, the Spanish capacity in rescue missions improved significantly. These planes arrived between May and November 1944 and were incorporated into the 51st Regiment based in Pollensa. The deployment in January 1945 was as follows:

Group	Aircraft	Number	Base
51 Escuadrilla	Dornier Wal	4	El Atalayón (Spanish Morocco)
51 Regimiento	He 59 He 60 Do 24T-3	2 5	Pollensa (Baleares)
54 Escuadrilla	Dornier Wal	2	Puerto de Las Palmas (Gran Canaria)
52 Grupo	He 114	11	San Javier (Murcia)
		24 (21 in service)	

As a curiosity, Spain had 1 Consolidated Catalina PBY-5A that was interned in Spain in July 1943 and acquired from its owner one year later. For various reasons, this aircraft did not start to be used before finishing the WW2.

CHAPTER VII

The Reconnaissance Groups

After the SCW, the EdA had different models numerous aircraft that had been used for reconnaissance tasks. Among them were German, Soviet or Italian origin aircraft such as the Heinkel He 45, Henschel Hs 126, Dornier Do 17 (in their versions P, E and F), Polikarpov R-Z „Natasha" and Caproni Ca.310. The tasks that had to be fulfilled were very important, especially in the areas of the northeast of the Iberian Peninsula and the Spanish Protectorate in North Africa.

After the selection of the airplanes that were in suitable conditions to serve in the EdA in 1939, they proceeded to its deployment in 3 Groups, an independent Squadron and a Patrol.

We have used the excellent work of González Serrano as the main source of information as well as various works by Arráez Cerda and the Historical Service of the Air Force and the Ministry of Defense on the study of the Air Force during the WW2 years.

In January 1940 the reconnaissance aviation deployment was as follows:

Unit	Aircraft	Number	Base
Grupo 41	He 45	18	Mola (Vitoria)
Escuadrilla 41	Do 17	8	Sanjurjo (Zaragoza)
Grupo 42	Ca.310	13	Villafría (Burgos)
Grupo 43	Polikarpov R-Z	34	Aumara (Larache)
Patrulla 41	Hs 126	5	Sania Ramel (Tetuán)
		78 (49 in service)	

During 1940 some changes were made in the reconnaissance aviation organization, such as the elimination of the 41st Squadron and the creation of the 44th Group. Due to this modification, the venerable Caproni Ca.310 and He 45 were left out of the reconnaissance aviation but not of active service in other branches of the EdA.

Thus, the deployment in January 1941 was as follows:

Unit	Aircraft	Number	Base
Grupo 43	Polikarpov R-Z	32	Aumara (Larache)
Grupo 44	Do 17	13	Sanjurjo (Zaragoza)
Patrulla 41	Hs 126	4	Sania Ramel (Tetuán)
		49 (24 in service)	

In the following years the main novelty was the incorporation of 5 ex Republicans Grumman GE-23s "Delfin" which had fled to Oran at the end of the SCW and that had finally been returned to Spain, as well as 4 more who had been abandoned at Catalonian aerodromes (northeastern region in Spain next to French border). These aircraft were assigned to the 41st Patrol from 1942. By the middle of 1945 the deployment of reconnaissance aviation was as follows:

Unit	Aircraft	Number	Base
Grupo 43	Polikarpov R-Z	9	Aumara (Larache)
Grupo 44	Do 17	13	Alcalá de Henares (Madrid)
Patrulla 41	Hs 126	3	Sania Ramel (Tetuán)
	Grumman GE-23	6	
		31 (17 in service)	

Despite their obsolescence, reconnaissance aircraft played an important role when it came to studying the movements of aircraft and troops in the border areas with Spain, without any air clashes with airplanes from belligerent countries.

CHAPTER VIII

The Transport Squadron

The need to have a transport unit made the 11 Squadron (which was originally a bombing unit) transformed into a transport and liaison unit, mainly in the Spanish Sahara.

The unit was created on September 1, 1939 and its equipment was several Ju 52 (4-5), 3 Bf 108 and 1 Fokker F-XII.

No other unit of greater size carried out transport tasks during the years of WW2.

CHAPTER IX

The Flight School

An imperative need in any air force is to train new pilots with the maximum demand in order to ensure the continuity and military aviation greater performance. In Spain after the SCW, in the middle of 1939, work was already being done to create the necessary infrastructure for this flight school.

The first allocation of aircraft for the Academy was composed of Savoia S.81 (11 copies), Caproni AP.1 (7 copies), Breda Ba.65 (10) and Heinkel He 70 (1). The following year in April 10 CR.32 and 3 González-Gil Pazó GP-1 joined the School. A mixture of various types of aircraft in small quantities was also used, as well as aircraft that were being withdrawn from frontline units.

In September 1939 the Flight Schools organization was completed, being divided into 2 Groups: Levante Group and South Group. Each of these Groups was in turn composed of 2 Elementary Schools and 1 Transformation School. In addition there were other independent schools such as Fighter, Crew, Blind flight and Specialists.

Although a small number of these magnificent airplanes were already available, from 1941 onwards, the aviation schools aeronautical park was finally improved thanks to the Spanish company CASA (Construcciones Aeronáuticas Sociedad Anónima), which began to deliver several aircraft (manufactured under the license of the German patent): Bücker Bü 131 (530 manufactured), Bücker Bü 133 (25 manufactured) and Gotha Go 145 (25 manufactured). Although the first Bücker Bü 131 aircraft had already arrived in Spain in 1936 and 1937, or the Gotha Go 145 in 1938, all of them acquired in Germany.

We have used the excellent work of González Serrano as the main source of information as well as various works by Arráez Cerda and the Historical Service of the Air Force and the Ministry of Defense about the Air Force study during the WW2 years.

The Fighter Schools deployment in the early 1940s was as follows:

Group	Unit	Base	Aircraft	Number
Grupo de Levante (Eastern Group)	Escuela elemental (Basic School) nº1	Alcantarilla (Murcia)	Bü 131 Bü 133C	35 1
Grupo de Levante	Escuela elemental nº2	El Palmar (Murcia)	D.H. 60GIII Moth Major Percival Gull Six D.H. 83 Fox Moth	3 1 1
Grupo de Levante	Escuela de Transformación (Transformation School)	San Javier (Murcia)	D.H. 82 Tiger Moth He 45 S.81 Hispano E-30 Ca. 310 Bü 131 Go 145 Ju 52 D.H. 60GIII Moth Major	3 19 5 8 4 1 1 4 7
Grupo Sur (Southern Group)	Escuela elemental nº1	El Copero (Sevilla)	Bü 131	18
Grupo Sur	Escuela elemental nº2	Las Bardocas (Badajoz)	Bü 131	19
Grupo Sur	Escuela de Transformación	Jeréz de la Frontera (Cádiz)	Bü 131 Bü 133C Ro.37bis Ju 52 S.81 Ar 66 Go 145 Ca.310	5 14 10 2 1 4 15 3
	Escuela de Caza (Fighter School)	Reus (Tarragona)	Cr.32 Ro.41 I-16 Caproni AP.1 Bf 108 Bf 109B GP-1 Cr.30 Ba.28	18 20 1 6 1 1 1 2 2
	Escuela de vuelo sin visibilidad (Blind Flight School)	Matacán (Salamanca)	Junkers W 34 Ju 52 He 111 GP-1	2 7 1 3
	Escuela de Tripulantes (Crew School)	Málaga	Ju 52 He 45 He 46 D.H. 82 Tiger Moth	2 3 6 3

			D.H. 60GIII Moth Major	9
			GP-1	1
Academia del Arma de Aviación (Air Force Academy)	León		Caproni AP.1	4
			CR.32	8
			He 70	1
			S.81	11
			Ba.65	10

Throughout the WW2 years there were slight changes in the in service aircraft number and models in the different Schools. There were also changes in the bases, as happened with the Fighter School that was transferred from Reus to Morón de la Frontera between July and October 1941. But it was not until July 1943 that the General Air Academy was founded.

CHAPTER X

The Meteorological Squadron

This unit was responsible for carrying out meteorological surveys and its official name was the Meteorological Probing Group based in Barajas (Madrid) and it was under command of the Ministry of Air Flight Protection General Directorate.

Following the superb work of Arráez Cerdá about this Squadron, we know that this unit always had the support of Germany, a country for which meteorological surveys were carried out. For example, the meteorological surveys in the area of the Bay of Biscay that were carried out between May and June 1940 were carried out by this unit and the information acquired was transmitted to the Germans who used it to their advantage both for their submarines fleet and for the Luftwaffe. This unit initially had 2 Ju 52 (who had served with identical mission in the Legion Condor), which were joined before February 1941 3 He 111J which were transferred to Spain to carry out meteorological surveys in support of Germany (these 3 airplanes were originally airplanes that were in charge of realizing liaison flights with the air company HISMA between Spain and Germany, and their names were Madrid, Seville and Barcelona). The close relationship of these aircraft with Germany was demonstrated when the revision made to He 111 25-102 (named Barcelona) was not carried out in Spain, but after taking off from Barajas (Madrid) they landed at the Bordeaux airport. Merignac, in occupied France, was in review for 15 days. On the return flight, the Spanish aircraft used the Luftwaffe badges, being replaced by the Spanish ones once it landed in Spain (a band with the colors of the Spanish flag at the tips of the wings and on the tail).

Other 3 He 111, on this occasion model H5, were „given" to Spain on December 29, 1943, with the same purpose. The planes, although Spanish-owned, were checked at German air bases in France, and piloted by Spaniards although the rest of the flight personnel were German.

CHAPTER XI

Other Units

In addition to the units that we have mentioned, there were other units within the EdA such as the Air Staff group, the flight experimentation units, the Regions and the Air Areas HQ squadrons, etc.

CHAPTER XII

Conclusions

The birth of the Spanish Air Force was determined by the recently ended clash between Spaniards in the SCW. After the SCW, Spain was destroyed and the population was exhausted, but had an Army with a large amount of weapons, numerous and well trained for the year 1939. The immediate start of WW2 took Spain in the process of reconstruction, which would still take years in completion; reason why immediately it was outphased in its armament in comparison with the belligerent countries.

We have been able to understand throughout the pages of this text the Spanish Air Force difficult birth, which, despite the large number of aircraft available to it, was obsolete in view of the numerous warlike advances of the WW2. Despite this and with a great effort of pilots and ground crew, the EdA could defend the skies of Spain and its African Protectorate of any belligerent aircraft, mainly Allies, although in some case from the Axis.

We have also remembered the Spanish participation in the WW2 air war in the Eastern Front thanks to the 5 Blue Squadrons. The Spanish pilots who fought against the USSR between October 1941 and March 1944 were not only part of the „payment" from Spain to Germany for the help received during the SCW by Franco's side (along with their comrades from the Spanish Army: the Blue Division), but also tried to learn as much as possible of the Luftwaffe to implement a new concept of air warfare in Spain, since the way of carrying out the air war during the SCW had become obsolete. Spanish pilots also allowed Spain to acquire, despite its neutrality, modern aeronautical material such as Ju 88 or Bf 109 F aircraft.

We have also recalled the large number of Allies and Axis aircraft that ended their flights on Spanish land or waters; and how many of them got back later into action inside the EdA.

Despite the unstable situation of non-belligerence/neutrality of Spain during WW2, it was the Spanish Army´s EdA branch that had the most confrontations with belligerent countries over Spanish land and waters.

Names as Hevia, Cuadra, Gavilán, Sánchez-Arjona, Aldecoa, Arango, Entrena, etc., will be written with golden letters in the memory of the Spanish Aviation because the great courage and combat spirit that demonstrated. For these reasons and despite the little known of their participation in the WW2, it is fair to pay tribute to them with this text in order to achieve that the Ejército del Aire (Spanish Air Force) history; pilots, crews, mechanics and soldiers become better known.

ANNEXES

Annex1: The Spanish Aeronautical Arsenal

As we have learned in the previous chapters, that the airplanes that constituted the EdA aeronautical arsenal was very heterogeneous. These aircraft generally came from four main sources: the National Aviation (which was the aviation belonging to the winning side in the SCW), the Legionary Aviation (the planes that the Italians had left behind in Spain after the SCW), the Legion Condor (the planes that the Germans had left in Spain after the SCW) and the Republican Aviation (which was the aviation belonging to the defeated side in the SCW).

All surviving SCW aircraft had fought well for the 1930s, but in the 1940s they were real antiques with fewer features than most German, American or British planes. Only the He 112 and the Bf 109 E in the fighters and the He 111 in the bombers could be considered aircraft with similar capabilities to those of other aviations, although only during the first year of the war since in 1940 they had already become outdated.

Another very important topic to consider is the state of conservation and maintenance of the EdA aircraft. Regarding the wear and tear of the airplanes, it is necessary to add that most of them had fought during the SCW and had several years of an intense use. In spite of the good work of the Spanish mechanics, managing to maintain these aircraft in flight conditions represented a great challenge for Spain after the SCW.

Finally we must remember that the Spanish political positioning in WW2 was very close to Germany and Italy (the old allies in the SCW of General Franco's side) and therefore these countries were where Spain tried to buy more modern aircraft. But the high wear and tear during the WW2 of Italy and especially Germany did not allow the Spanish desires to acquire new aircraft to come to fruition when and as Franco wished. During the WW2 Germany did not sell large amounts of war material to other countries being always very reluctant, due to the need for weapons for the German Army; so they resisted these sales or established high prices to prevent or at least delay the acquisition of military equipment. When Germany finally agreed to sell military equipment, it did so mainly with countries allied with Germany (Hungary, Romania, Slovakia, Finland or Italy); but with neutral countries the airplanes or armored vehicles sale was much more limited. Finally, Spain managed to convince the German Reich to sell it aircraft in exchange mainly for strategic materials and operational aids (rather than money). But from 250 day fighters, 75 night fighters and 150 bombers that Spain wanted, only a few fighters and bombers would be acquired by the EdA.

In this section we will discuss the most important models and we will refer to their origins, features and qualities.

Messerschmitt Bf 109: From the Legion Condor that were transferred to the EdA in their models A, B, E-1 and E3. There were finally 27 copies left in Spain.

In 1943, 15 Bf 109 F2/F4 fighters (previously used by Luftwaffe units) were purchased from Germany at a price of 202,000 marks per aircraft. The Bf 109 F were denominated in Spain "Zacuto". These very valid aircraft were delivered at the French airfield in Villecoubley where they were picked up by Spanish pilots (who had been transferred in a Ju 52 belonging to the EdA and from the Iberia airline). At the same aerodrome, the 15 planes were tested by the 15 Spanish pilots under the command of Lieutenant Colonel Manso on May 15, 16 and 17. Finally, on May 17, 1943, they took off towards Chateaurox, where they only landed 14 Bf 109Fs, since one had to make an emergency landing near Poitiers (the pilot was unharmed) that did not allow the plane to be repaired. From Chateaurox they took off on the 17th with a new stop in Toulouse. On the 18th they took off from Toulouse, making a stopover at the Reus Air Base (in Tarragona, near the Pyrenees) on 19th. Subsequently, they continued their flight to the south, stopping on 21st at the Barajas airbase (in Madrid) to continue the fly to their destination: the Morón aerodrome (in Seville) where the 14 Bf 109Fs landed on May 22. Although initially they were deployed in the Tablada airbase along the 22nd Fighter Regiment to help the pilots belonging to the last two Blue Squadrons to fly aircrafts similar to those that could be used in Russia. Later (in 1945) they would be trasfer gradually to the 23rd Fighter Regiment in Reus, closer to the French border.

Fiat G.50: Several copies of this aircraft that were purchased from the Regia Aeronautica and grouped in the Tablada aerodrome (Seville). Between July 17 and 20 the Spanish pilots (who had piloted the Fiat Cr.32 in SCW) were learning everything possible from the manuals for the handling of these Italian aircraft. On July 20 began the flight tests with Super Fiats, as they were called these aircraft in Spain. They were later transferred to the 27th Group of the EdA under the command of Commander Guerrero that was deployed in Nador along with the Heinkel He 112. The G.50s formed the 27th Group 2nd Squadron whose symbol was a greyhound jumping down inside a white circle.

These aircraft suffered various problems in the landing gear during their service in North Africa and flew fewer flight hours than their He 112 "brothers".

Polikarpov I-16: 21 I-16s captured to the Republican Aviation were recovered at the end of the SCW, to which 30 more I-16s were added that were assembled in a workshop with pieces prepared for that purpose.

Heinkel He 112: 19 were acquired by the National Aviation during the SCW in three rounds. The first in December 1938, the second in early 1939 and the third just after the SCW. The 15 surviving aircraft were deployed in the 27th Group in Nador and formed the 1st Squadron of the 27th Group whose symbol was a greyhound jumping upwards inside a black circle.

Fiat Cr.32: This fighter had been the main "workhorse" of the National Aviation during the SCW. Due to the great service provided during the SCW, 100 were manufactured with license in Spain by Hispano-Suiza in Tablada (Seville) and were delivered between 1940 and 1942. The main problem with this maneuverable airplane is that in 1939 it was underarmed and underpowered.

NAME	OFFICIAL CODE	NUMBER	YEAR OF ARRIVAL TO AVIACIÓN NACIONAL/EdA	ORIGIN	ARMAMENT	ENGINE
Messerschmitt Bf 109 A (one crew)	6	14	1938-39	Germany	2 7.92 mm machine guns	Junkers Jumo 210B 631 HP
Messerschmitt Bf 109 B (one crew)	6			Germany	2 7.92 mm machine guns	Junkers Jumo 210G 700 HP
Messerschmitt Bf 109 E-1 (one crew)	6	27		Germany	4 7.92 mm machine guns	DB 601 1100 HP
Messerschmitt Bf.109E-3 (one crew)	6			Germany	2 cannons 20 mm + 2 7.92 mm machine guns	DB 601 1100 HP
Messerschmitt Bf 109 F-2/F-4 (one crew)	6 Zacuto	15	1943	Germany	1 cannon 20 mm + 2 7.92 mm machine guns	DB 601 E 1.350 HP
Fiat G.50 (one crew)	1	12	1939	Italy	2 12.7 mm machine guns	FIAT A 74 625 HP
Polikarpov I-16 (one crew)	1W	51	1939	USSR	2 cannons 20 mm + 2 7.92 mm machine guns	Shvetsov M-63 1100 HP
Heinkel He 112 (one crew)	5	15	1938	Germany	2 cannons 20 mm + 2 7.92 mm machine guns	Junkers Jumo 210Ga 700 HP
Fiat Cr.32/ Hispano HA-132L (one crew)	3	+124/100	1937	Italy	2 12.7 mm machine guns	FIAT A 30 600 HP

Heinkel He 51: 30 specimens of this obsolete assault airplane survived the SCW. Here we have to add another 15 He 51 when the SCW had finished. Finally it was possible to have a total of 49 He 51 in January 1940. The models of this airplane in the EdA were A-1, B-1 and C-1.

Henschel Hs 123: After the SCW Spain, it was able to fly 14 Hs 123 that had been sold by Germany to the National Aviation. The cost of each plane was RM 86,511.33. These aircraft were already considered obsolete from the WW2beginning, since in the letter that Air Minister Juan Yagüe wrote to Generalissimo Francisco Franco in February 1940 in which he indicated his desire to sell the less useful aircraft (some of these useless planes were the Henschel). For various reasons, the Henschel continued in service with the EdA for many years, as they retired in 1953. During the WW2 years, there were two accidents with the Hs 123 while they belonged to the 61 Squadron.

Polikarpov I-15bis or I-152: These planes came from the captured ones to the Republican side after the SCW. It seems that 21 airplanes were recovered, although in the EdA there is only the delivery of 20. After finishing the WW2 they were scrapped.

Heinkel He 114A: 12 hydroplanes were acquired in Germany in 1943 and were destined to the Alcázares Seaplane Base.

Dornier Do 24T-3: in 1944 EdA acquired 12 Dornier Do 24T3 destined to perform search, rescue and rescue tasks; so they lacked weapons. As usual, a group of pilots and crew was sent to carry out a rescue and management course for Dornier in Étang de Berre (in Occupied France) with Seenotstaffel 3. This was carried out between May 21 and 30 of 1944 in the French Berre lake. Between 30th of May and 15th of August, the first 5 planes departed towards Pollensa (where they had been destined to carry out their rescue tasks in Mediterranean waters). The remaining 7 Dornier arrived in Pollensa in September (3), October (3) and November (1). Operations of the Do-24 over the Mediterranean began in 1944 summer, always in close coordination with the countries involved to avoid incidents.

The first Do 24T-3 arrived in Mallorca on May 30, and that same day it had its first mission to save a Luftwaffe pilot on the sea whose plane had been shot down near the border between France and Spain (near of Port Vendres). On the trip back to Mallorca, with the German pilot rescued, two RAF Beaufighters intercepted the Spanish plane, although they did not attack him when he saw the Spanish insignia and the Red Cross symbol that carried the plane.

Dornier Do 17: From 32 Do 17s who fought in the SCW, 13 survived the combats (5 of the P model and 8 of the E and F models) and joined the EdA.

NAME	OFFICIAL CODE	NUMBER	YEAR OF ARRIVAL TO AVIACIÓN NACIONAL/EdA	ORIGIN	ARMAMENT	ENGINE
Heinkel He.51 B (one crew biplane)	2	49	1937	Germany	2 7.9 mm machine guns	BMW VI 500 HP
Henschel Hs 123 (one crew biplane)	24	14	1937	Germany	2 7.9 mm machine guns 450 kg bombs	BMW 132 CDc 880 HP
Polikarpov I-15bis/I-152 (one crew biplane)	2W,8	20	1939	USSR	2 12.7 mm machine guns	M-25 V 775 HP
Heinkel He 114A (two crew seaplane)	61	12	1943	Germany	2 7.9 mm machine guns	BMW 132K 974 HP
Dornier Do 24T-3 (5-6 crew seaplane) (seaplane)	65	12	1944	Germany	------	3 BMW Bramo 323 R-2 1000 HP
Dornier Do 17 P (4 crew)	27	5	1938	Germany	3 7.9 mm machine guns	2 BMW 132N 875 HP
Dornier Do 17 E-F (4 crew)	27	8	1938	Germany	3 7.9 mm machine guns 500 kg bombs	2 BMW VI 7.3 740 HP

Savoia S.79: After the SCW were 30 S.79s the survivors who could be deployed in the EdA. This aircraft was used throughout WW2 by the Regia Aeronautica or the Aeronautica Nazionale Republicana due to its great value, but since 1939 it can be considered as an obsolete aircraft.

Savoia S.81: These obsolete aircraft of Italian manufacture, after being incorporated to the National Aviation in 1937 were withdrawn very soon from the EdA, since in 1942 they were not in the list of the Spanish combat planes.

Heinkel He 111: 58 copies were received from the Legion Condor. The Heinkel He 111s were models B and E. This bomber can be considered that in 1939 had not been completely obsolete, although new models were already used by the Luftwaffe.

Subsequently, 3 He 111J (in 1941) and 3 He 111H (in 1943) were purchased from Germany to carry out meteorological surveys in support of Germany. The airplanes belonging to the Meteorological Squadron in Barajas, which depended on the Flight Protection General Directorate of the Ministry of Air.

Fiat Br.20: 13 copies of this venerable Italian-made airplane fought with the Legionary Aviation. Of the 13 aircraft, 10 survived the SCW and were delivered to the EdA.

Tupolev SB-2: 25 planes of these bombers belonging to the Republican Aviation were reunited after the SCW, of which 18 entered service with the EdA. Another example of an airplane that had been very advanced when it was manufactured but was completely obsolete in the first years of WW2.

Junkers Ju 88: After many attempts, Spain finally got a modern bomber and high combat capacity as the Ju 88 A4 at an approximate price of 600,000 marks each of the 10 aircraft that were purchased (the purchase contract was signed on November 12, 1942 and according to this, Spain should supply raw materials to Germany equivalent to 6900000 marks). 20 pilots and bombers-machine gunners along with 30 mechanics belonging to the EdA were sent to France, where they arrived on July 7, 1943. There they received a transformation course for the new plane at the Francazal aerodrome (Toulouse) because unlike what happened with the Bf 109, the Spaniards did not previously have Ju 88s and therefore it was necessary to learn to pilot them. At the same aerodrome aircraft were delivered on November 30, 1943. The 10 aircraft (whose previous owner had been the IV/KG76 of the Luftwaffe) arrived in Spain on November 30, 1943 on a nonstop flight to Los Llanos Air Base in Albacete, being deployed in the 13th Bomber Regiment in February 1944.

To these Ju 88 there have to be added more copies due to the incorporation of several planes that had been interned when landing in Spain. At least 21 Ju 88 of various types were those who for various reasons had to land in Spain and be interned. Of the 21 Ju 88 at least 13 were put in flight conditions (4 Ju 88 A, 5 Ju 88 D, 2 Ju 88 C6 and 2 Ju 88 T) while another 5 were left for training and spare parts. The interned airplanes were bought to Germany in February of 1944 and all were incorporated into 13th Bomber Regiment (Albacete).

Since 1943, in addition to the acquisition of Ju 88s and Bf 109s, Spain acquired the manufacturing license for Bf 109G, He 111 and Ju 52. Other materials of great military interest were also purchased, such as 88-caliber anti-aircraft guns (at least 88 copies). and a anti-aircraft guns manufacture license, four landing radio beacons, 10 Würzburg FuG 39 TD radioteleometers, a "Freya" radiolocalizer and three "Liechtenstein" location devices. These were the first radars in service in Spain and represented an important advance in regarding the defense of Spanish air space (they were deployed near Madrid).

NAME	OFFICIAL CODE	NUMBER	YEAR OF ARRIVAL TO AVIACIÓN NA- CIONAL/EdA	ORIGIN	ARMAMENT	ENGINE
Savoia S.79	28	62	1937	Italy	2 12.7 mm machine guns 2 7.7 mm machine guns 1 20 mm cannon 1200 kb bombs	3 ALFA ROMEO 128 RC-18 860 HP
Savoia S.81	21	15	1937	Italy	6 7.7 mm machine guns up to 2000 kg bombs	3 ALFA ROMEO 125 RC35 680HP

Heinkel He 111 B	25	22	1939	Germany		2 DB 600C 1000 HP
Heinkel He 111 E	25	36	1939	Germany	4 7.9 mm machine guns 2000 kg bombs	2 Jumo 211A-1 1000 HP
Heinkel He 111 J	25	3	1941	Germany	4 7.9 mm machine guns 2000 kg bombs	2 DB 600CG 1000 HP
Heinkel He 111 H	25	3	1943	Germany	7 7.9 mm and 1 13 mm machine guns 1 20 mm cannon	2 Jumo 211F 1340 HP
Fiat Br.20	23	10	1939	Italy	3 12.7 mm machine guns 1600 kg bombs	2 FIAT A80 RC-41 1000 P
Tupolev SB-2	20W	18	1939	USSR	4 7.62 mm machine guns 600 kg bombs	2 Klimov M-103 1000 HP
Junkers Ju 88 A-4	29	10	1943	Germany	4 7.9 mm machine guns 3000 kg bombs	2 Junkers Jumo 211J 1420 HP

Annex 2: Aircraft Used By Expeditional Squadrons

The Spanish Expeditionary Squadrons or Blue Squadrons had the opportunity to fly different aircraft models while fighting in the skies of Russia.

There were four main aircraft models: Messerschmitt Bf 109 E7, Messerschmitt Bf 109 F4, Focke Wulf Fw 190 A3 and Messerschmitt Bf 109 G6. All the planes were the same as those used by other units of the Luftwaffe, although it is true that when the Spaniards used the E model, some Luftwaffe units already used the F; or when the Spanish used the F, and some German units used the Fw 190.

We comment below the main characteristics of these 4 aircraft:

Messerschmitt Bf 109 E7: the Spanish pilots of the 1ˢᵗ Squadron managed to adapt more easily to this Bf 109 model since during the SCW it was already used in Spain. In addition the EdA had several Bf 109 E1 and E3, so there were several pilot officers who already knew about the use of the plane.

With the Messerschmitt, the Spaniards had an airplane that could carry out both fighter and escort missions as well as ground attacks.

The E7 was a "long range" version of the E4 (which in turn was a version of the E3 with improved weaponry of Oerlikon MG-FF/M guns in each wing and with a higher rate of fire), with the capacity to mount a 300 liters drop tank.

Messerschmitt Bf 109 F4: Possibly this aircraft valuing its performance and firepower was the best Bf 109 of all the models manufactured (later the models increased their weight with the new engines and weapons systems, reducing their maneuverability). F4 was the F series most used version.

This model of the Bf 109 was used by the Spaniards as a pure fighter, which was for the mission for which they were manufactured.

Focke Wulf Fw 190 A3: The 3rd and 4th Blue Squadron had the opportunity to use these powerful German aircraft. The Fw 190 was characterized by its great maneuverability, high top speed, great structural strength, very powerful weaponry and a Plexiglas cabin that allowed great visibility. Its four guns and two machine guns had a devastating effect against enemy planes, something that the Spaniards did not take long to check. The progress from Bf 109 F model to Fw 190 was very important for the Spanish pilots since they could fly a completely different airplane to the Messerschmitt and that the EdA did not possess; allowing in this way to increase the learning of the Spaniards.

Messerschmitt Bf 109 G6: This Bf 109 was the result of Germany's need for aircraft with greater speed to deal with enemy aircraft. The power and speed increase in the Bf 109 resulted in the aircraft being heavier and reducing its maneuverability in order to gain speed and horizontal acceleration. It was the most important Bf 109 version and was made as an armaments platform, being able to install field modifications or "Rüstsätse" in the front aerodromes.

NAME	SQUADRON	ARMAMENT	ENGINE
Messerschmitt Bf 109 E7	1st	2 20 mm cannons + 2 7.92 mm machine guns	Daimler-Benz DB 601 A 1.175 HP
Messerschmitt Bf 109 F4	2nd y 3rd	1 20 mm cannon + 2 7.92 mm machine guns	Daimler-Benz DB 601 E 1.350 HP
Focke Wulf Fw 190 A3	4th	4 20 mm cannons + 2 7.92 mm machine guns	BMW 801 D-2 1700 HP
Messerschmitt Bf 109 G6	5th	1 30 mm cannon + 2 13 mm machine guns	Daimler-Benz DB 605 A 1.475 HP

Annex 3: Belligerent Aircraft Interned In Spain

Throughout the years of the world conflict, there were many planes from both the Allies and the Axis, which were interned in Spanish territory. Obviously the geographical situation of Spain and its many coasts kilometers, allowed many aircraft from WW2 participating nations that came very close or even flew over Spanish airspace. There are different records of the different airplanes interned in Spain in the Spanish Air Force Historical Service and on the website "Españoles en la 2ª Guerra mundial" that have served as the main sources for the preparation of this annex and Annex 4 too. The different geographical areas that witnessed these aerial incidents were:

- Cantábrico (northern Spain): in this geographical area, both the allied planes (belonging to the RAF, US Navy and USAAF) and the German planes flew to hunt submarines and enemy ships. Although it was not necessary to penetrate the Spanish airspace, it is known that in many cases the Spanish Cantabrian coast (and especially the Biscay Bay) was overflown at low altitude by various types of aircraft, both Allied and German. The Spanish Government was forced to protest officially on many occasions, despite which these flights continued to occur. The encounters between the planes from both sides and their enemies caused some aircrafts to be damaged in combat and forced to land in Spain.

Recall that the return of the German submarines to their French west coast bases began to be exclusively made by outlining the Spanish coast, where they could more easily mislead the Allies radars. Besides, the Luftwaffe pursued allied convoys in the Atlantic and protected its submarines in the Cantabrian Sea.

- Levante and Baleares (eastern Spain): since the beginning of WW2 the l'Armee de l'Air French airplanes began to appear on the Spanish Levantine coast. In many cases the airplanes moved from their aerodromes in France to those in North Africa, and for mechanical problems they basically ended up in Spanish territory better than crashing into the sea. Later also some Italian and Vichy France planes flew close to Spain. Some of these Italian aircraft participated in attacks against the Gibraltar British base (in Spanish territory) and returned damaged and run out of fuel to the southern France Axis bases.

- Strait of Gibraltar (between south of the Iberian Peninsula and north of Africa): the presence of an Allied military base as important as Gibraltar, led to many planes from both sides flying over these lands and Spanish jurisdictional waters. From the beginning of "Operation Torch" the number of airplanes that overflew this geographical area increased a lot and, therefore, in many occasions they ended up landing in better or worse flight conditions, in Spanish territory.

- Canary Islands: as we discussed above, the Canary Islands were the objective of the Allies almost from the beginning of the war and following the "Operation Torch" the transit of Allied planes through the Canary skies increased giving rise to several incidents.

The causes for which these aircraft ended in Spain were very varied, the main ones being the following:

- planes that were lost and landed in Spain.
- damaged or shot down airplanes after a battle that took refuge in the nearest territory.
- airplanes with technical problems or running out of fuel that forced them to force landing.
- other causes.

There is a long-winded official documentation about these airplanes interned in Spain, although very possibly they were more than those mentioned in this text.

Once these aircraft arrived in Spanish national territory or jurisdictional waters, their destinations were different fundamentally according to their usefulness and conservation degree:

- some were incorporated into the Spanish air fleet (when acquired in their countries).

- others were scrapped.

- another group was disassembled and stored.

In the same way, the conditions of conservation and functioning in which they arrived were very different, as some were in perfect flight conditions, others needed repairs and another group arrived in such bad conditions that it was completely useless to try to put them in flight again.

In general, the Allied or Axis planes pilots and crews that landed in Spain were interned in some combatants meeting centers, although in many cases they were allowed some freedom. In other cases, they were interned in military concentration camps, such as Miranda de Ebro. Despite this, many Axis and Allied pilots and crews were able to return to their countries and continue flying during the war. In November 1942, after the "Operation Torch" by which the Allies landed in North Africa and after the bombing suffered in La Linea (Cádiz) by Italian aircraft mistake in October 1942, the performance of the Spanish Government with the Italian and German planes that landed in Spain changed radically. From that moment, the crews were repatriated but the planes were interned.

It is important to emphasize that from signing the armistice in France, and the subsequent call to resistance by Charles de Gaulle on June 18, 1940, many pilots of l'Armee de l'Air ended up on Spanish land.

In the following list we will name most of these planes that were interned in Spain with their date, type of plane, nationality, place and fate of the plane after being interned. In some cases that are more interesting, we will briefly tell these planes story that finally led them to be interned.

DATE	AIRCRAFT	COUNTRY	PLACE	FATE
VI -18-1940	LeO 451	Armee de l'Air	Oliva, Valencia.	Aircraft burned, Interned crew.
VI -18-1940	Potez 540	Armee de l'Air	Porto Cristo, Mallorca	Airplane disassembled and stored. Interned crew.
VI –19-1940	Martin 167-F	Armee de l'Air	cerca de Valencia	Airplane disassembled and stored.
VI –19-1940	LeO 451	Armee de l'Air	Almería	Airplane disassembled and stored.
VI –20-1940	Mureaux 117	Armee de l'Air	San Carlos de la Rápita	Aircraft repaired and stored.
VI –20-1940	Bloch MB 174	Armee de l'Air	San Luis (Menorca)	Aircraft repaired and stored.
VI –21-1940	Potez 63-11	Armee de l'Air	Son San Joan (Mallorca)	Aircraft repaired and acquired by Spain (EdA).
VI –21-1940	Bloch 220	Armee de l'Air	Manises (Valencia)	Aircraft repaired and stored.
VI –23-1940	Bloch MB 174	Armee de l'Air	Mahón (Menorca)	Aircraft repaired and stored.
VI –25-1940	Potez 540	Armee de l'Air	Sabadell (Barcelona)	Airplane disassembled and stored.
VI –26-1940	Caudron C-630	Armee de l'Air	Algeciras	Aircraft repaired and acquired by Spain (EdA).

VII –9-1940	Savoia S.79	Regia Aeronautica	Menorca	Aircraft repaired and returns to Italy

DATE	AIRCRAFT	COUNTRY	PLACE	FATE
III –9-1941	Swordfish MK.I	Royal Navy	Islas Canarias	Aircraft repaired and acquired by Spain (EdA).
V-1941	Bristol Beaufighter	272 Sqdn. de la RAF	Jerez	Aircraft stored and interned crew.
VI-15-1941	Fw 200	I/KG 40 Luftwaffe	Navia (Asturias)	Aircraft repaired by German mechanics and repatriated 3 days later.
VII-5-1941	Fw 200	3/KG 40 Luftwaffe	Tablada (Sevilla).	Aircraft repaired by the crew and return to Bordeaux.

The Swordfish MK.1 seaplane, license plate P4073 from 700 Sqdn. and belonging to the battleship HMS Malaya carried out surveillance and merchant ships convoys protection on III-9-1941 in the air area between Gibraltar and Freetown. This plane had to hurry his flight a lot, so it ran out of fuel and had to land near of the Canary Islands.

A Spanish merchant ship called "Cabo de Buena Esperanza" picked up its 3 crew members and the plane, transferring them to Santa Cruz de Tenerife.

As was usual, the crew was interned (later in 1942 it was repatriated to Great Britain).

The seaplane was in perfect working condition, so it was stored at first and then, on February 15, 1944 the Spanish Government bought the Swordfish MK.1 along with a Blenheim and a Beaufighter for 1,200,000 pesetas. Once acquired in Great Britain, the seaplane was repaired in 1944 and joined the Seaplane 54 Squadron, with the numeral HR6-1, until in 1946 it was discharged and scrapped.

The day VI-15-1941, 3 Focke Wulf FW 200 Condor I/KG 40 (based on the French Atlantic coast) were damaged by attacking a convoy in the Cape St. Vincent maritime area. On the return flight due to the several damages, one of them crashed in Portugal but another one with the numeral F8 + FH, landed in Navia (Asturias). The landing must have been complicated due to the size and aircraft damage and the airstrip short length (about 500 meters). The Ltn. Otto Gose decided to land in Spanish territory because they run out of fuel, as well as the death of the flight mechanic. Immediately in the Condor base arrived the information about the airplane landing in northern Spain and a Ju 52 with spare parts, fuel and technicians was sent, who repaired the airplane and took the crew member corpse. Only 3 days after the landing, the Condor returned to its base.

DATE	AIRCRAFT	COUNTRY	PLACE	FATE
1942	2 Do-24	Luftwaffe	Camariñas (Galicia)	Aircrafts repaired and return to their base in France.
IV-30-1942	Swordfish	RN	Entre Ras el Farea y Punta Pescadores	Interned aircraft.

VI-28-1942	P.108B	274 Squadriglia Autonoma Regia Aeronautica	Los Alcázares (Murcia)	Aircraft repaired, interned and later scrapped.
VI-28-1942	P.108B	274 Squadriglia Autonoma Regia Aeronautica	Palma de Mallorca	The aircraft replenished and returned to his base in Sardinia.
VI-28-1942	P.108B	274 Squadriglia Autonoma Regia Aeronautica	Valencia	Destroyed in forced landing.
VI-29-1942	S.79	Regia Aeronautica	Los Alcázares (Murcia)	The aircraft replenished and return to Italy.
VI-29-1942	S.79	Regia Aeronautica	Puig (Valencia),	Destroyed in forced landing.
VI-29-1942	S.79	Regia Aeronautica	Son San Juan (Baleares)	The aircraft replenished and return to Italy.
X-11-1942	Ju-88D-1	Luftwaffe	Playa de la Hípica, Melilla	Airplane disassembled and stored.
X-27-1942	Ju-88D-1	Luftwaffe	Son San Juan (Baleares)	Aircraft interned and acquired by Spain (EdA).
X-1942	Cant Z.1007Bis	Regia Aeronautica	Palma de Mallorca	Avión destrozado en aterrizaje.
XI-6-1942	Ju-88D-I Trop	Luftwaffe	Alcantarilla (Murcia)	Aircraft interned and acquired by Spain (EdA).
XI-8-1942	C-47-DL	USAAF	Zeluán (Protectorado español en África)	Aircraft interned and acquired by Spain (EdA).
XI-8-1942	C-47-DL	USAAF	Villa Sanjurjo (Alhucemas)	Aircraft interned and acquired by Spain (EdA).
XI-8-1942	C-47-DL	USAAF	Tetuán (Protectorado español en África)	Aircraft interned and acquired by Spain. Iberia (Spanish airlines). adquires the aircraft.
XI-17-1942	Blenheim Mk.V	RCAF	Mazarrón (Murcia).	Unknown.
XI-1942	Blenheim	RAF	Cerca de Tánger.	Unknown. Interned crew.
XII-23-1942	P-38 Lightnings	USAAF	Cerca de Gibraltar	Unknown.
XII-27-1942	Airacobra P-400	USAAF	Tánger	Aircraft interned.
XII-1942	He-111	6/KG26 Luftwaffe	Cubelles near Barcelona	Airplane disassembled and stored

On VI-28-1942 there was a night attack on the Gibraltar base by several Regia Aeronautica 274 Squadriglia Autonoma BRG (Bombardamento a Grande Raggio) Piaggio P.108B. Due to the large distance from its base to Gibraltar, the increase in fuel consumption caused several aircraft to have difficulty returning to their starting aerodrome. The P.108B with numeral MM-22007, landed at the Palma de Mallorca, airport where it refueled and returned to its base in Sardinia. Another P.108B, with numeral MM-22005, landed at the Los Alcázares aerodrome (Murcia) and was interned and after some tests its use was discarded, being finally scrapped at the end of the war. A third P.108B, with numeral MM-22001, crashed and destroyed when trying a forced landing in a Valencian beach.

The IX-8-1942, a USAAF group belonging to the 12th Air Force transported paratroopers in direct flight from England to Oran to support the "Operation Torch". Three Douglas C-47-DL of the formation run out of fuel and their pilots thought who were on French territory, landed in the Zeluán, Villa Sanjurjo and Tetuán Spanish aerodromes.

The three planes and their occupants were interned, being housed in the Legión barracks in Nador, being repatriated to Gibraltar shortly after (February 1943).

Due to the high Spanish interest in the three modern transport planes, their acquisition was negotiated at a price of 100,000 dollars each, with the purchase taking place on December 10, 1943. The three aircraft were converted to the DC-3 version (with between 21 and 28 seats), they entered service in Iberia in July 1944 to carry out flights on the Barcelona-Madrid-Lisbon and Seville-Tánger-Tetuán-Melilla airlines.

DATE	AIRCRAFT	COUNTRY	PLACE	FATE
I-1-1943	Fw 200 C-4/U3	8/KG40 Luftwaffe	Sevilla	Interned aircraft and used by the EdA.
I-1-1943	Fw 200 C-4	8/KG40 Luftwaffe	¿?	Unknown.
I-1943	B-25D-10	USAAF	Nador (Melilla)	Interned aircraft then repaired and bought by Iberia.
II-25-1943	B-24D-1-CO	USAAF	Spanish Protectorate in Morocco	Airplane damaged when landing. Interned crew.
III-24-1943	Ju 88 C-6	Luftwaffe	La Albericia (Santander)	Interned aircraft.
IV-2-1943	Ju-88D-1 Trop	Luftwaffe	Mallorca	Interned aircraft and used by the EdA.
IV-7-1943	Ju-88A-14	Luftwaffe	Mallorca	Interned aircraft and used by the EdA.
IV-19-1943	P-38	USAAF	Melilla	Interned aircraft.
V-1943	Douglas Boston III	RAF	Vejer de la Frontera	Aircraft with no damage but destroyed when it was flown again. Interned crew.
V-17-1943	B-24D-30-CO	USAAF	Agoncillo? (Logroño)	Unknown.
V-20-1943	Ju-88A-4	III/KG30 Luftwaffe	San Salvador Beach (Tarragona).	Airplane disassembled and used by the EdA.
V-20-1943	He-111H-11	5/KG26 Luftwaffe	Son San Juan (Mallorca)	Interned aircraft and used by the EdA.
V-23-1943	B-26B-10-MA	USAAF	Uad Xebica. Spanish Protectorate in Morocco	Interned aircraft, then scrapped.
V-27-1943	Ju-88	2(F)./123 Luftwaffe	Manises (Valencia)	Aircraft destroyed.

VI-19-1943	S.70	Regia Aeronautica	Alcalá de Henares (Madrid)	Interned aircraft.
VI-28-1943	P-38G	USAAF	Nador	Interned aircraft, then scrapped.
VII-1943	Grumman Avenger TBF-1	US Navy	Cádiz	Interned aircraft.
VII-1-1943	Ju 88 C-6	Luftwaffe	La Albericia	Unknown.
VII-4-1943	Ju-88D	Luftwaffe	Ibiza	Unknown.
VII-7-1943	Catalina	USAAF	Sidi-Ifni	Interned aircraft then repaired and used by the EdA.
VIII-13-1943	FW 200	9/KG 40 Luftwaffe	Camariñas	Airplane, disassembled and stored.
VIII-15-1943	P-38G-15-LO	USAAF	Menorca	Unknown.
VIII-18-1943	Ju-88A-14	III/KG26 Luftwaffe	Reus	Interned aircraft and used by the EdA.
VIII-27-1943	Ju-88A-14	KG26 Luftwaffe	Mallorca	Interned aircraft and used by the EdA.
VIII-1943	Ju-88T	1(F)./123 Luftwaffe	Mallorca	Airplane damaged when landing Unknown.
IX-1943	BV 138C-1	1./S.A.Gr.129 Luftwaffe	Vizcaya	Scrapped.
IX-1943	S.81	Regia Aeronautica	Barcelona	Interned aircraft and returned to Italy at the end of the war.
IX-1943	S.81	Regia Aeronautica	Barcelona	Interned aircraft and returned to Italy at the end of the war.
IX-1943	S.81	Regia Aeronautica	Mallorca	Interned aircraft and returned to Italy at the end of the war.
IX-9-1943	5 Romeo Ro.43	Regia Aeronautica	Mallorca (4) Pollensa (1)	Interned aircrafts, bought to Italy and used by the EdA.
IX-9-1943	Ro.44	Regia Aeronautica	La Alcudia	Interned aircraft, bought to Italy and used as Ro.43 spare parts.
X-9-1943	B-24D-110	USAAF	Sevilla	Unknown.
X-15-1943	Fw 200 C-4	7/KG 40 Luftwaffe	Santiago de Compostela	Interned aircraft and used by the EdA then by Iberia.
XI-11-1943	He-111H6	I/KG26 Luftwaffe	Los Alcázares	Unknown.
XII-20-1943	B-24D-30-CO	USAAF	Spanish Protectorate in Morocco	Unknown.

Eleven KG 40 Focke Wulf Fw 200s, took off from Bordeaux on December 30, 1942 to bomb Casablanca. Two of the planes, hit by anti-aircraft artillery, tried to reach Spain. The first day of 1943 one of the two damaged aircraft, specifically the Fw 200 C-4/U3 with numeral F8+AS belonging to 8/KG40, when trying to return to its base the pilot considered that it was impossible and that the best option was to land in Seville. As was usual, there was no problem for the crew to be repatriated in just a few days. The airplane did stay in Spain, to later enter into service in the Spanish Air Force. That same day, another Condor airplane with numeral that participated in the same bombing, also had an emergency landing in Spain.

The same January 1943 an USAAF B-25D-10 Mitchell that flew from Gibraltar to Tunisia, has problems with the rudder and had an emergency landing in the Nador aerodrome (although the pilot thought that was already on French territory). In that aerodrome it was stored until the end of the WW2, when finally the Spanish Government acquired the airplane. In 1948 it was put in flight condition after laborious maintenance work, being used as training aircraft in the Air Force from 1950 to 1953.

On May 20, 1943, two Luftwaffe planes landed in Spain. A Junkers Ju-88A-4 with numeral 4D+KS and belonging to III/KG30 after a combat mission had to make an emergency landing on the San Salvador beach (Tarragona). After being interned, it was dismantled and sent to the Maestranza Aérea (Air Force facilities) in Albacete, where it was used as a training plane. The other plane was a He-111H-11 with numeral 1H+CN belonging to 5/KG26, that during the performance of its mission in Mediterranean waters, it ran out of fuel to reach its base, so the pilot decided land at the Son San Juan aerodrome (Mallorca). The airplane was interned and was incorporated to the Air Force Meteorological Squadron in June of 1945.

Only three days later, an USAAF B-26B-10-MA landed in Uad Xebica. His compatriots immediately went to rescue them, but the arrival of the Spaniards prevented the plane from returning to its base. The plane subsequently made a trip to Madrid, stopping at Larache and Tablada; although at the end of WW2 it was finally scrapped.

On 7/7/1943, an USAAF Consolidatcd PBY-5A OA-10-CO seaplane was mistakenly landed in the Sidi-Ifni Spanish territory. The modern seaplane was in perfect condition so it interested to the Spanish Government, which after the negotiation with the American Embassy was acquired for Spain at the end of the war.

In November 1943 a BV 138C-1 seaplane belonging to the Luftwaffe 1./S.A.Gr.129 based in Biscarosse, on the French Atlantic coast during a surveillance flight ran out of fuel near its base with the crew being picked up by another German seaplane, while the plane had to be retrieved by a German ship. But before the German ship arrived the sea took it near of the Vizcaya coasts, being dragged by some Spanish fishermen who moved it to the Lekeitio harbor. The plane was left there in Barakaldo waiting to decide its fate, although finally in 1946 it was scrapped.

After the Italian armistice in September 1943, several Italian pilots tried to flee with their planes. A seaplanes flight (assigned to the Italian cruisers from the naval group headed by the Roma battleship) composed of 5 Romeo Ro.43 and 1 Ro.44 departed from the La Spezia base on September 9, 1943, several hours after to know officially the armistice between Italy and the Allies news. The pilots decided to go to the Baleares Islands; in particular, four of them landed in the Palma bay, another one in Pollensa and the last one in the Alcudia base. The seaplanes were interned until August 1944 when they were bought to Italy for 355,317 pesetas. Later they entered service with the EdA in 1946 within the 51st Seaplane Regiment.

DATE	AIRCRAFT	COUNTRY	PLACE	FATE
II-5-1944	B-24H-10-CF	USAAF	Villa Cisneros (Marruecos español).	Aircraft repaired and crew repatriated.
IV-29-1944	B-24H-10-CF	USAAF	Barcelona	Unknown.
V-21-1944	Ju-88T1	1.(F)/33 Luftwaffe	San Javier (Murcia)	Unknown.
VI-5-1944	S.79 III	Aeronautica Nazionale Repubblicana	Castelldefells	Airplane destroyed when landing, disassembled and stored.
VI-5-1944	S.79 III	Aeronautica Nazionale Repubblicana	Tarragona	Airplane, disassembled and stored.
VI-5-1944	S.79 III	Aeronautica Nazionale Repubblicana	Reus	Interned aircraft.
VI-25-1944	B-24H-15-FO	USAAF	Palma de Mallorca	Unknown.
VI-27-1944	B-17 G-10-VE	KG 200 Capturado por la Luftwaffe	Manises (Valencia)	Interned aircraft, then sold and scrapped.
VII-12-1944	B-24	USAAF	Barcelona?	Interned aircraft for 11 days
VII-12-1944	Ju-88A-17	III/KG77 Luftwaffe	Mallorca.	Unknown. Crew repatriated.
VII-24-1944	B-24H-10-DT,	USAAF	Barcelona	Unknown.
VII-1944	Ju-88P	Luftwaffe	Reus	Interned aircraft and used by the EdA.
IX-14-1944	B-25D-35	USAAF	Palma de Mallorca	Unknown.
X-20-1944	Halifax Mk.V	520 Sqdn. RAF	Marruecos español.	Unknown.
XI-1944	P-51D-15-NA	USAAF	Cidamón (La Rioja)	Unknown. Pilot repatriated.
IV-6-1945	Ju 290 A5	Lufthansa	Barcelona	Interned aircraft.
IV-23-1945	S.82	Aeronautica Nazionale Repubblicana	Barcelona	Interned aircraft.
V-1945	Siebel SI-204-A	Luftwaffe		Airplane used by the German embassy in Spain.

In June 5 early morning, three planes belonging to the Aeronautica Nazionale Repubblicana had to land in Spain due to engines problems and because they ran out of fuel. These aircraft had participated in a night attack on Gibraltar and belonged to a 9 Italian Savoia S.79 III aircraft group from the French Istres base. One was badly damaged when landing on the Castelldefells beach, fortunately leaving the crew unharmed (the plane wreckage was collected and moved to Sabadell); a second S.79 III landed in the Ebro delta area (Tarragona) and was also destroyed (the plane wreckage was collected and moved to Sabadell); and the third plane landed unharmed in Reus.

The war and the difficulty of returning the planes to the Italian Social Republic, make the Italians negotiate with Spain the sale of the same, although without success. Finally the two S.79 III that were in Spanish territory after finishing the WW2 were returned to Italy.

On June 27, 1944, a curious incident took place in the skies of Spain, as a B-17 G-10-VE was interned when having to make an emergency landing when ran out of fuel at the Manises aerodrome in Valencia. The B-17 belonged to the Luftwaffe KG 200 since it was a plane captured at the USAAF. The B-17 carried out a transport mission for three German spies a former member of the French Foreign Legion and an Arab from Marseilles, with the aim of transporting them to North Africa for secret missions. The plane was interned in Manises with the German badges covered, until the end of the war to be later scrapped.

On April 6, 1945, with the war in Europe almost ending, a Lufthansa airline Ju 290 A5 that was flying the Berlin-Barcelona line tried to land with an intense fog at the El Prat airport, having to abort the landing and try again. Finally it had to land on a secondary airstrip suffering slight damage.

Annex 4: Belligerent Aircraft Accidents In Spanish Land

In the same way that many airplanes were interned in Spain during WW2 as we have related in the previous annex, in many occasions the planes that arrived at land or Spanish jurisdictional waters, did it only to crash. In these cases the crew members were killed or injured in many cases, while the planes were destroyed and only served to be sold as scrap in some cases.

We relate below these aircraft relationship with their date, type of aircraft, nationality, place and plane final destination. In some more outstanding cases, we will briefly describe the events that ended with the plane crash.

DATE	AIRCRAFT	COUNTRY	PLACE
VI-22-1940	LeO 451 B4	Armee de l'Air	Pirineo de Huesca
VIII-30-1940	Do-17	Luftwaffe	Güeñes (Vizcaya)
IX-26-1940	He-111	Luftwaffe	Playa de Sevares (Asturias)
III-27-1941	Vickers ?	57 Sqdn RAF	Formentera
VI-20-1941	Bristol Blenheim	105 Sqdn RAF	Finisterre
VI-20-1941	Vickers Wellington	RAF	Águilas (Murcia).
VII-30-1941	Blenheim Mk.IV	110 Sqdn RAF	Tarragona?
XII-16-1941	Hudson	24 Sqdn RAF	La Coruña
XII-21-1941	Fw200C-3/U4	I/KG 40 Luftwaffe	Cantabria
I-2-1942	Fw200C	KG40 Luftwaffe	Ría de Camariñas (Galicia)
I-9-1942	Vickers Wellington	RAF	Punta Europa

I-21-1942	Consolidated Catalina	RAF	Tarifa
IV-1942	Beaufighter Mk.VIc	236 Sqdn RAF	Punta Umbria (Huelva)
IV-19-1942	Swordfish	813 Sqdn RN	Alborán
VI-1942	Beaufighter	235 Sqdn Coastal Command	Costa de Málaga
VI-12-1942	Whitley Mk.V	58 Sqdn RAF	La Coruña
VII-12-1942	Fw200C	KG40 Luftwaffe	Ría de Muros
VII-14-1942	Bristol Beaufort Mk.II	RAF	Motril (Granada)
VII-20-1942	Wellington	RAF	Islas Sisargas
VII-20-1942	Ju-88C-6	III/KG 40 Luftwaffe	Lagosteira
VIII-20-1942	Lancaster I	RAF	A Pontenova
VIII-20-1942	Ju-88C-6	Luftwaffe	Lagosteira
VIII-28-1942	Wellington	RAF	Huelva
IX-25-1942	Catalina Mk1B	119 Sqdn RAF	Golfo de Cádiz
X-3-1942	Wellington	RAF	Fuerteventura (islas Canarias).
X-10-1942	3 Spitfires Mk.Vb	52nd Fighter Group USAAF	Melilla
X-11-1942	Spitfire Vb	RAF	Cabo Sacratif (Granada)
X-23-1942	Wellington Mk.1C	RAF	Gran Canaria
X-1942	Wellington	RAF	Protectorado español de Marruecos
XI-1-1942	Hudson	233 Sqdn RAF	Islas Baleares
XI-8-1942	Halifax	78 Sqdn RAF	Valencia
XI-11-1942	C-47	64th TCG USAAF	Tetuán
XI-15-1942	P-38F	27th FS USAAF	La Coruña
XI-18-1942	Fw200C	Luftwaffe	Barcelona
XI-1942	Blenheim	18 Sqdn RAF	Alicante
XI-21-1942	Stirling Mk.I	15 Sqdn RAF	Platja d´Aro
XII-11-1942	Whitley	10 OTU RAF	Asturias
XII-13-1942	Ju-88D-1	1(F)/33 Luftwaffe	L'Escala (Gerona).
XII-15-1942	B-24	301 FTU RAF	Rota (Cádiz)
XII-27-1942	Lockheed Hudson	500 Sqdn RAF	Santa Pola (Alicante)
XII-27-1942	Lockheed Hudson Mk.IIIA	233 Sqdn RAF	Alicante

On March 22, 1940, a LeO 451 B4 bomber belonging to the Groupement du Bombardement 6 de l'Armee de l'Air departed from its Lézignan base (near Narbonne and the Leon Gulf coast) headed towards the French territories in North Africa overflying mainland. Unfortunately, although we do not know the cause, it finally crashed in the Pyrenees (in the province of Huesca).

A Vickers Wellington of the No. 1 Overseas Aircraft Despatch Unit based in Portreath, made a flight from England to Gibraltar on July 20, 1941. The fuel consumption increased during the flight so that it ran out of fuel when flying over the coastal area next to Murcia. Then it sank in front of El Fraile island, in Águilas (Murcia).

The plane was practically destroyed, despite which it was tried to tow to the mainland, although it finally sank. Little was taken advantage by the Spaniards of the wreckage of the British plane.

The Fw 200 Cs omnipresent in the Atlantic waters in search of freighters or enemy warships were the protagonists of several incidents. Specifically, on January 2, 1942, a Condor belonging to the KG 40 located HMS Scottish in front of Cabo Espiche. The plane immediately prepared to make an attack pass on the enemy ship, although in the course of the attack it was shot by the antiaircraft artillery from HMS Scottish. The damages received were very important, so the pilot decided to land in the Camariñas estuary (in Galicia), where it sank. Thanks to the pilot's skill, neither he nor the rest of the crew suffered significant damage, so they were initially interned in Spain shortly after being repatriated to the Reich. Here we can take notice about the Spanish permissiveness during the first years of the WW2 as related to the internment of clashed belligerent aircrafts crews.

During the WW2, there were innumerable flights that made Allied planes to transfer from a Theatre of Operations to other one. In April 1942 a Bristol Beaufighter Mk.VIc belonging to 236 Sqdn. RAF (along with 11 other planes also from the same Squadron) was ordered to move to the Middle East to reinforce the 272 and 252 Sqdn. RAF. The flight was long and required a stopover at the Gibraltar airfield. The difficulty of the long journey and possibly to the atmospheric conditions motivated them that four of the twelve planes did not arrive in Gibraltar (one of the 8 that arrived, crashed when trying to land). One of them, crashed near the beach of Punta Umbria (Huelva). The two crews of the plane died being buried in the British cemetery of Huelva.

On July 20, 1942 there was a meeting in the skies near the Galician coast between 2 RAF Wellingtons belonging to the 15 OTU (which were making a transfer flight from Great Britain to the Middle East) and 1 Ju 88 C6 belonging to the III / KG 40. The clash between the 3 aircraft occurred near of the Sisargas Islands (near Malpica de Bergantiños). The result of the combat was the one Wellington shot down by the Junkers (two crew members died and the third was rescued by a Spanish fishing vessel) and the shot down of the Ju 88 by the other Wellington (both Luftwaffe crew members died).

A month later in the same area a Lancaster I of the RAF belonging to 61 Bomber Sqdn. but temporarily assigned to the Coastal Command carried out tasks of search of a German merchant ship called Wesserland, which transported Wolfram from Spain to the German occupied Europe (remember that the Wolfram was one of the elements accepted by the Germans for the payment of the debt that Spain had with Germany). While the Avro Lancaster continued its search on the Galician waters, two German Ju-88 C6 located it then shot down the British plane (although several seconds before the British could shot down one of the attackers Ju 88 C6). As we can see, these clashes between one or two planes of both sides occurred relatively frequently over territorial waters and even over Spanish land.

DATE	AIRCFRAT	COUNTRY	PLACE
I-28-1943	Halifax	RAF	Ceuta
II-5-43	P-400	350th FG USAAF	Navia (Asturias)
II-6-43	He-111	II/KG26 Luftwaffe	Alborán
II-21-43	Wellington	179 Sqdn RAF	Cabo Juby
II-21-43	Ju-88D-1	1(F)/122) Luftwaffe	La Manga (Murcia)
III-43	2 Hawker Hurricane	253 Sqdn RAF	Manacor
III-12-43	Hudson VI	RAF	Algeciras
IV-1943	Hurricane	32 Sqn RAF	Baleares
IV-1943	Catalina Mk1B	210 Sqdn RAF	Cabo Toriñana (Galicia)
IV-5-1943	B-26B-2 Marauder	452 BS USAAF	Galicia
IV-19-1943	Ju-88D-1 Trop	1(F)./122)Luftwaffe	Pollensa
IV-27-1943	Bell P-39D-BE	?	Punta Umbria (Huelva).
V-17-1943	Withley	RAF	Finisterre
V-19-1943	Martin B-26C-15-MO	USAAF	Spanish Morocco
V-30-1943	Whitley	RAF	Finisterre
VI-9-1943	Catalina Mk1B	RAF?	Tarifa (Cádiz)
VI-12-1943	P-40L	USAAF	Marruecos Español
VI-12-1943	B-26C-10	USAAF	Sahara español
VI-13-1943	Sunderland	228 Sqdn RAF	Finisterre
VII-1943	Sunderland	204 Sqdn RAF	Mauritania-Canarias
VII-7-1943	Beaufighter	RAF	Galicia
VII-10-1943	Ju-88C-6	Luftwaffe	Finisterre
VIII-17-1943	B-24	480th AG USAAF	Finisterre
VIII-25-1943	Do-217 E-4	IV/KG-2 Luftwaffe	Espot (Lérida)
IX-4-1943	PB4Y-1 Liberator	USAAF	Finisterre
IX-4-1943	Ju-88C-6	13/KG40 Luftwaffe	Galicia
IX-29-1943	Boeing B-17E	206 Sqdn Coastal Command RAF	Punta Carnero
X-3-1943	Douglas Boston III	1th OADU RAF	Tarifa
X-1943	Spitfire PR Mk IX	10 ADU RAF	Huelva
X-21-1943	Ju-88	1.(F)/121 Luftwaffe	Baleares
XI-11-1943	Mosquito PR.IX	544 Sqdn RAF	Peña
XI-11-1943	Sunderland Mk.III	228 Sqdn RAF	?
XI-19-1943	2 Vickers Wellington	Operational Training Unit RAF	Cabo Ortegal
XII-5-1943	B-17E	68th RG USAAF	Cabo de Creus
XII-28-1943	PB4Y-1	VB-103 US Navy	Jerez
XII-1943	Ju 290 A-3	Luftwaffe	Lesaca (Navarra)
XII-1943	P-47D-10-RE	27 ATG USAAF	Mendata (Vizcaya)
I-14-1944	Beaufighter	404 Sqdn RCAF	Cabo Trafalgar
II-6-1944	Spitfire Mk.Vb	RAF	Spanish Marruecos
II-19-1944	Junkers Ju 290	2./FAGr 5(11) Luftwaffe	La Coruña
II-22-1944	C-47A	USAAF	Tarifa
III-1944	B-26C-30-MO	14 Sqdn RAF	Mataró
III-1944	B-17G-10	452 BG/728 BS USAAF	Zaragoza
III-10-1944	Ju-88C-6	7/KG40 Luftwaffe	Cabo de Peñas

III-24-1944	Ju-88A1	II/KG30 Luftwaffe	Pirineos
III-27-1944	B-24	44th Bomb Group USAAF	Bilbao
III-28-1944	Avro Anson	SAAF	Sahara Español
IV-1-1944	Do-217E-5	III/KG100 Luftwaffe	Isla de Cabrera
IV-18-1943	Spitfire PR Mk IX	RAF	Larache
IV-20-1944	Bristol Beaufighter Mk X	235 Sqdn RAF	Golfo de Vizcaya
V-1944	Ju 290 A7	Luftwaffe	Brañueta
V-12-1944	Ju-88A-17	III/KG77 Luftwaffe	Ibiza
VI-3-1944	Sunderland	RAF	Fernando Poo (Guinea Ecuatorial)
VI-15-1944	Catalina MkIVA	RAF	Melilla
VI-19-1944	B-17G-10	401BG/610BS USAAF	Lequeitio (Vizcaya)
VI-25-1944	B-17G-45	91st BG USAAF	Erandio
VI-25-1944	B-17G-35-DL	379th BG/524th BS USAAF	Roncesvalles
VII-1944	Beaufighter Mk VI	414th NFS USAAF	Llanás (Gerona)
VIII-15-1944	Halifax B.II,	624 Sqdn RAF	Palamós
VIII-15-1944	Do-217M-11	7./KG100 Luftwaffe	?
VIII-18-1944	Catalina MkIVA	RAF	Tarifa
1944	Douglas A-26B-15-DT Invader	USAAF	Laxe (Galicia)
V-29-1944	2 Grumman Wildcat FM-2/F4F	VC-55 US Navy	Islas Canarias
V-8-1945	He-111H-23	Luftwaffe	San Sebastián

During the year 1943 and 1944, although the incidents continued in northern Spain waters, the Mediterranean Theater of Operations witnessed a significant increase in the number of incidents with belligerent planes in Spanish waters and lands.

On February 5, 1943, a Bell P-400 of the 347th USAAF Fighter Squadron (350th FG) that made a transfer flight from Predannack along with 4 other P-400s and was destined for Port Lyautey (French Morocco) run out of fuel, which motivated him to make an emergency landing in Navia (Asturias). The pilot could not prevent the plane from crashing, suffering important damages that did not allow to repair it. The plane wreckage was sent to the Cuatro Vientos aerodrome (Madrid).

The Germans also used Spanish airspace for their missions. On February 21, 1943 a Ju 88 D1 of 1 (F)/122, was hit by enemy fire while it was during a reconnaissance mission over the western Mediterranean (the Junkers had its base in Sardinia). The airplane damages were very important and the pilot tried to land near the beach of La Manga (Murcia), although they were not lucky and the three crew members died.

Approximately one month later 2 Hawker Hurricanes of 253 Sqdn. (RAF) (which was based near Philipville (Algeria) from where they flew as convoy escort, patrols over the sea), arrived in Mallorca during a mission to protect the "Windsor Castle" ship that was transporting troops. The planes lost their course and one pilot made a forced landing near Manacor, while the other pilot bailed out into the same area.

Both pilots survived and were interned in the center prepared for such mission that existed in Alhama de Aragón.

Another Ju 88 D1 belonging to 1 (F). 122 during the reconnaissance flight in the North African area on April 19, 1943 run out of fuel. The pilot tried to solve the problem seeking protection in Spain, specifically in the Balearic base in Pollensa. Although he was finally unable to land at the aerodrome, he did make a forced landing on a cereal field, almost destroying all the plane (its remains were dismantled and sent to Albacete). The four crew members saved their lives and were repatriated two days later without problems.

The two following incidents had Finisterre (in Galicia) as a witness. The first incident occurred on June 13, 1943 when a Short Sunderland of 228 Sqdn (RAF), was shot down by the German U-564 submarine antiaircraft artillery. This submarine along with the U-185, U-358, U-564, U-634 and U-653 had been discovered by the RAF aircraft, but managed to defend themselves without suffering losses. Two months later the B-24 belonging to the 480th Antisubmarine Group known as "Bessie, The Contented Cow" after an air crash with two Fw 200C Cóndor, was damaged, having to land at Playa Langosteira (Finisterre). Before being shot down, the B-24 knocked down one of the Fw 200Cs.

Again, a Short Sunderland Mk.III seaplane from the 228 Sqdn (RAF) while carrying out the attack on the U-966 German submarine was shot down by three Luftwaffe JU-88 C-6 off the northern Spanish coast.

Another airplane that in March of 1944 looked for ships that transported Tungsten (Wolfram) from Spain to the occupied Europe was a B-26C-30-MO belonging to the 14 Squadron (RAF). While carrying out its maritime reconnaissance mission, it crashed in front of Mataró (northeast of Spain) without the causes being known. That same month, but on the Spanish north coast, a Ju 88 C6 belonging to 7/KG40 was shot down over Cabo de Peñas by a Mosquito of 248 Sqdn. (RAF) during the fight around the Japanese submarine I-29.

On March 28, 1944, a VIP transport Avro Anson belonging to the SAAF, took three RCAF commanders from Marrakech to Agadir and was lost due to a sandstorm. With the confusion, they ran out of fuel so the pilot landed, although in the Spanish Sahara. The plane was not damaged when it landed but was looted by the locals, rendering it unusable. The crew and passengers were repatriated quickly, since the course of the war had modified the Spanish Government attitude in this topic.

At the end of the war there were many III Reich high commands who tried to escape and avoid the capture by the Allies. One of them was León Degrelle (who became head of one of the SS Divisions) and fled in He-111H-23 with numeral TQ+MU (it was Albert Speer's personal plane). In his flight the pilot tried to get away as much as possible from the Europe newly liberated by the Allies and reach Spanish ground, where the Franco regime would provide them with help. The fuel of the plane lasted only until the Spanish coast in San Sebastian, crashing on La Concha beach and run out of fuel. There are two pictures of this plane in the book, whose remains were taken the next day to the facilities of the Lasarte airfield, and finally ended up in the Air Force Facilities in Logroño.

Annex 5: Spanish Air Force Badges And National Emblems

In this section, we will comment on the Spanish aircraft insignias during WW2, making a distinction between those used by Spanish aircraft in Spanish territory and that about aircraft piloted by Spaniards in the skies of the USSR (Blue Squadrons or Escuadrillas Azules).

In Spain, after the SCW, the airplanes of the winning side used black round badges on both sides of the fuselage (although sometimes in the interior was painted the Falange's symbol with the Yoke and Arrows). These black badges were painted from August 8, 1936 replacing the tricolor badge in order to avoid unwanted mistakes and shot downs to be confused with the insignia of the Republican side (red-yello-red Vs. red-yellow-purple). On the wings, black round or black diagonal cross insignia were commonly used. The tail was painted on a white background, a St. Andrew's Cross or a Burgundy's Cross (similar to the cross used in the Bulgarian Air Force during WW2 when it was an Germany's ally). The St. Andrew's Cross, represents the martyrdom to which the apostle was subjected and its use in Spain dates back to the time of the marriage of Joan of Castile with Philip the Beauty, being attached to the Spanish shield the Burgundy's Cross, region where Saint Andrew is the patron, as a tribute to her husband.

After finishing the SCW and with the creation of the Air Force, the SCW period insignias were maintained, although with some modifications. Although it was already used during the SCW in some occasions, after the SCW it began to generalize the use of the national red-yellow-red cockade (yellow). This consisted of a circle with the three colors of the Spanish national flag: red in the outside ring - yellow in the middle ring - red in the inner disc) in 4 positions on the wings and sometimes on both sides of the fuselage (although the black circle continued to be used).

The use of the national yellow red badge was necessary to highlight the Spanish nationality of every airplane that carried it and thus avoid being confused with belligerent countries airplanes (during the text we could verify that in some cases, Spanish airplanes were confused with aircraft belonging to the Italian Regia Aeronautica for example) since Spain used airplanes mainly from Italian and German origin.

The St. Andrew's Cross continued to be used in the tail until today.

The Blue Squadron aircrafts used the same insignia as the Luftwaffe aircrafts; the swastika or Hakenkreuz in the tail and the Balkenkreuz in the fuselage and the wings. In addition, the Spanish aircraft also used the Theater of Operations marks, which consisted of painting the nose and wingtips of the planes in yellow, as well as the yellow band on the fuselage. The Spaniards Ju 52s that were used on the Eastern Front, used German insignia as well. The only significant difference with the other Luftwaffe planes on the Eastern front was the insignia of each of the Blue Squadrons on the fighter´s nose, although this badge was not used on all planes.

Despite belonging to JG 27 and JG 51, we have not seen any photographs where the emblems of either JG are observed on Spanish planes. The badge that was the symbol of the 5 Blue Squadrons, was the Joaquín García Morato´s Fighter Group badge (leader of the national fighter branch aviation during the SCW). But each Squadron made some modifications, so there were 5 badges that were used by the Blue Squadrons.

In the nose of the 1ˢᵗ Squadron Bf 109 E, the mechanics painted the Joaquín García Morato's Fighter Group badge accompanied by a number two in Roman (II). That II indicated that it was the second struggle of the members of the famous unit against communism, since they had previously faced each other during the SCW. There are photographs where the use of this emblem is observed.

In the 2ⁿᵈ Squadron Bf 109 E, the Joaquín García Morato's Fighter Group badge was kept, although on a red Santiago Cross (Saint Jacques). Santiago Apostle is the patron of Spain, so it was decided to use his cross. There are photographs where the use of this emblem is observed.

The 3ʳᵈ Squadron again used the Joaquín García Morato's Fighter Group badge, although superimposed on a German Cross or Balkenkreuz (same as that used by the Luftwaffe planes). The WW2 and the changes in the planes used by the Spanish pilots, made that finally this emblem was not used in the nose of the fighters.

In the 4ᵗʰ Squadron, the omnipresent Joaquín García Morato's Fighter Group badge was placed on the emblem of the German Fighters (a winged arrow, surrounded by a laurel wreath). As it happened with the 3ʳᵈ Squadron, finally this emblem was not used in the nose of the fighters.

The 5ᵗʰ Blue Squadron, despite its brief period of action on the Eastern Front, also had its own emblem, which was the same as that of the 1ˢᵗ Squadron, the Joaquín García Morato's Fighter Group badge, but in this case accompanied for a 5 (Roman V) substituting II.

The Joaquín García Morato´s Fighter Group badge, a white circle with three birds in the center (a hawk, a bustard and a blackbird) and the phrase "Vista, suerte, al toro" that means "Sight, luck and towards the bull". The hawk represented García Morato, the bustard to Bermúdez de Castro and the blackbird, to Julio Salvador (the three Fighter Group founders). The phrase "Sight, luck and towards the bull" was a sentence used by bullfighters when entering the Bullfighting Ring to face the insecurity of their fate. They never knew if they would leave there alive. Everything depended on his Sight, his Luck and his Decision; and the pilots thought that in their air combats they would need the sight, the luck and the decision.

Annex 6: Spanish Air Force Ranks And Equivalences

We recall in this annex the equivalences between the ranks of the Spanish Air Force, the Luftwaffe, USAAF and RAF.

EJÉRCITO DEL AIRE	LUFTWAFFE	USAAF	RAF
Capitán General	Generalfeldmarschall	General (5 stars)	Marshal of the RAF
General del Aire	Generaloberst	General (4 stars)	Air Chief Marshal
Teniente General	General der Luftwaffe	Liutenant-General	Air Marshal
General de División	Generalleutnant	Major-General	Air Vice-Marshal
General de Brigada	Generalmajor	Brigadier-General	Air Commodore
Coronel	Oberst	Colonel	Group Captain
Teniente Coronel	Oberstleutnant	Lieutenant-Colonel	Wing Commander
Comandante	Major	Major	Squadron Leader
Capitán	Hauptmann	Captain	Flight Lieutenant
Teniente	Oberleutnant	First Lieutenant	Flying Officer
Alférez	Leutnant	Second Lieutenant	Pilot Officer
		Flight Officer	Warrant Officer
Suboficial Mayor	Stabsfeldwebel	Master Sergeant	Flight Sergeant
Subteniente	Oberfeldwebel	Technical Sergeant	Sergeant
Brigada	Feldwebel	Staff Sergeant	
Sargento	Unteroffizer	Corporal	Corporal
Cabo 1º	Obergefreiter		Leading Aircraftman
Cabo	Gefreiter	Private 1st Class	Aircraftman 1st Class
Soldado	Flieger	Private 2nd Class	Aircraftman 2nd Class

Annex 7: Blue Squadrons Air Victories

The 5 Blue Squadrons from October 1941 to March 1944 remained in the battle-front for almost 30 months. During these months they carried out 4944 combat missions, with 611 battles against the enemy and managed to shoot down 164 Soviet aircraft. On the negative side, the Spanish squadrons had 19 pilots killed and/or missing in combat, a prisoner pilot, 4 ground echelon soldiers dead and several different gravity injured.

Many of its pilots and ground staff received Spanish and German decorations and awards due to their courage and bravery during the months in which they fought in Russia.

Among the Spanish pilots there were 13 aces (when 5 enemy planes were shot down, the pilot was considered an Ace), although the short period of time in which each of the 5 Blue Squadrons fought in Russia, prevented the number of planes shot down by the Spanish pilots were as high as that of their German comrades. It is also necessary to remember that several pilots had flown during the SCW and had achieved several aircrafts shot down before going to Russia, but most of the pilots had no previous combat experience. The most outstanding pilots were Captain Hevia (3rd Squadron, 12 aircrafts shot down), Commander Cuadra (4th Squadron, 10 aircrafts shot down), Lieutenant Sánchez-Arjona (4th Squadron 9 aircrafts) and Captain Gavilán (3rd Squadron, 9 aircrafts shot down).

It is important to remember that although apparently the number of aircrafts shot down is not very high (in comparison with countries belonging to the Axis such as Romania, Italy, Bulgaria or Finland), the Blue Squadrons were organized following the pilots rotation principle. For this reason the combat service periods were only several months, which together with the bad weather in many times in the USRR, prevented the number of planes shot down by the Spanish was not very high.

A fact to remember (according to Caballero) is that the Germans consented to lend their planes to pilots belonging to a country that was not at war. Also as stated above, the Germans really appreciated and respected the Spanish pilots, their bravery and flying virtuosity, having fought together with them during the SCW.

Rank	Pilot	Blue Squadron	Aircrafts shot down in SCW	Aircrafts shot down in Russia	Others
Capitán	Hevia Álvarez de Quiñones	3rd	-	12	
Comandante	Cuadra Medina	4th	-	10	
Capitán	Gavilán Ponce de León	3rd	-	9	
Teniente	Sánchez-Arjona Courtoy	4th	-	9	Dead 19 Nov 1943
Alférez	Aldecoa Lecanda	3rd/4th	-	7	
Teniente	Arango López	2nd	-	7	
Comandante	Salas Larrazabal	1st	16 + 1/3	6	2 in ground
Teniente	Azqueta Brunet	3rd	-	6	
Teniente	Sánchez-Tabernero de Prada	4th	-	6	
Teniente	Valiente Zárraga	4th	-	6	
Teniente	Lucas Fernández-Peña	4th	-	6	
Capitán	Alós Herreros	3rd	-	5	
Capitán	Bengoechea Menchaca	2nd	-	4 (1 probable)	
Teniente	Meneses Orozco	3rd/4th	-	6	(2 with 4th BS)
Teniente	Barañano Martínez	2nd/3rd	-	4	(2 with 3rd BS)
Alférez	Mateos Recio	4th	-	4	
Teniente	Pérez Muñoz	3rd	-	4	
Teniente	Martínez Vara de Rey	3rd	-	4	

Capitán	Llaca Álvarez	4th	-	4	
Teniente	Cavanilles Vereterra	4th	-	4	Missing 10 Jan 1944
Comandante	Ferrándiz Arjonilla	3rd	-	3	
Teniente	Calleja González-Camino	3rd	-	3	
Capitán	Bayo Alesandri	1st	11	3	1 in ground
Capitán	De Frutos Rubio	2nd	2	2	
Alférez	Beriaín Arbilla	2nd/3rd	-	2	
Alférez	Guibert Amor	3rd/4th	-	2	(1 with 4th BS)
Teniente	Escalante de la Lastra	4th	-	2	
Alférez	Chicharro Lamamie de Clairac	4th	-	1	Dead 21 Aug 1943
Teniente	Ibarreche Arriaga	1st	7	1	
Capitán	Serra Pablo-Romero	2nd	3+1/3	1	
Teniente	Garret Rueda	2nd/3rd	-	1	
Teniente	Pérez González	3rd	-	1	Dead 8 Jun 1943
Teniente	Escudé Gisbert	2nd	-	1	
Teniente	Arango López	2nd	-	1	
Teniente	Arraiza Goñi	2nd	-	1	
Teniente	Medrano de Pedro	2nd	-	1	
Alférez	Bengoa Cremades	2nd/3rd	-	1	
Teniente	Luca de Tena y Laso	3rd	1	1	
Teniente	Lacruz Cuervo	3rd	-	1	
Teniente	Roselló Simonet	3rd	-	1	Dead 5 May 1943
Teniente	Serra Alorda	4th	4	1	
Teniente	Zorita Alonso	1st	-	-	1 in ground

The aircrafts shot down by each of the Blue Squadrons, according to the work of Arráez Cerdá and Caballero were:

SQUADRON	SHOT DOWN PLANES	PERIOD	PILOTOS	CASUALTIES
1st	10 + 4 in ground	Oct 1941-Dec 1941	17	6
2nd	13	Jun 1942-Nov 1942	19	2
3rd	62 (+1 Hevia in a german Staffel)	Dec 1942- Jul 1943	20	6
4th	74	Jul 1943- Jan 1944	20	10
5th	0	Feb 1944- Mar 1944	14	1
	159 + 1 + 4		90	25

Another very important matter that we must keep in mind is the rival skill that the Spanish pilots met in the skies of the USSR. We have already commented that at the beginning of the USSR invasion by Germany, the Soviet pilots have not the same skill as those belonging to the Luftwaffe. This fact was changing step by step during the war, but since 1943, the Soviet pilots behavior in the air combats was much better. To this topic we must add the aircraft that the Soviets mainly used until 1942-1943 and from that moment, since they used obsolete aircraft such as I-153, I-16 or LaGG-3, then to pilot aircraft with higher performance (which became superior to German aircraft when the Soviet pilot got an adequate performance) such as LaGG-5, La-5, Yak-9, etc. The Spanish pilots belonging to the Blue Squadrons could experience these changes in Soviet air power between 1941 and 1944 and witness how it was most difficult to shoot down enemy planes. In spite of their disadvantage, the pilots belonging to the 3rd and 4th Blue Squadrons managed to shoot down many Soviet planes, because the possibility of a clash with the Soviets increased a lot during the year 1943.

During the text we have narrated many of the Spanish pilots air victories, although not all. And we have known as the largest number of Spanish-Soviet air clashes, they were with fighters; in a second place with attack aircraft (such as Il-2) and in a lesser number of cases, with bombers.

The shot down types of planes by the different Blue Squadrons, based on the work of Arráez Cerdá:

	1st	2nd	3rd	4th	5th	Total
I-16	1					1
I-18	2 + 2 (ground)					4
DB-3	5	1				6
Pe-2	1	3	10 + 1 (Hevia)	2		16 +1
LaGG-3		6	26	26		58
Il-2		3	15	19		37
LaGG-5/La-5			6	22		28
Yak-1			3	1		4
I-153			1			1
Boston				3		3
Balloon				1		1
Otros	1 + 2 (ground)		1			2 + 2

The value of the Spanish pilots, who composed the different Blue Squadrons was endorsed by the citation even in one of the Orders of the Day corresponding to JG 51 when celebrating the 6,000 air victories (according to Carlos Caballero):

"For more than a year now, our Spanish pilots have been at our side, motivated by a will to fight tirelessly, surpassing each and every one of the many difficulties that have arisen in their path." With all their enthusiasm, they have contributed to the JG 51 achieves the successes of which we are proud. „

As we have related in this text and according to Caballero Jurado, the brave behavior of the military belonging to the different Blue Squadrons, allowed these Spaniards who fought together with Germany in the air war in Russia were awarded by the German

Reich: they received a German Gold Cross, 74 2nd and 1st class Iron Crosses, 571 Merit of War Crosses and 65 silver and bronze flight Pins.

In Spain the men of the Blue Squadrons received several Individual Military Merit Medals, 38 War Crosses with Palms and 27 got a new rank. But much more important was the military career of many of them that allowed them to become important ranks within the Army. Thus, the 1st Blue Squadron commander, Ángel Salas became Capitán General and several of the pilots achieved the Lieutenant General or General ranks. Also these pilots became the Spanish pilots elite after WW2, although that already belongs to another era that will not be reported in this text.

Bibliography

ABC. La eficacia de las baterías antiaéreas en Canarias en la II Guerra Mundial. 2007.

Aeroplano nº 29. 100 años de la Aviación Militar Española. IHCA. 2011.

Angelucci, Enzo; Matricardi, Paolo, Pinto, Pierluigi. " Complete book of World War II Combat Aircraft". White Star Publishers. 2001.

Abellán García-Muñoz, Juan. Galería de aviones de la Guerra Civil española (1936-1939). Ministerio de Defensa. 2003.

Almenam Editorial.

Arráez Cerdá, Juan. Fiat G.50 en Espagne. Air Magazine 22. 2004.

Arráez Cerdá, Juan. Les Espagnols de la Luftwaffe. Les Escadrilles Bleues. Ciel de Guerre 18. 2010.

Arráez Cerdá, Juan. Les Espagnols de la Luftwaffe. Les Escadrilles Bleues. Ciel de Guerre 19. 2011.

Arráez Cerdá, Juan. Les He 111 méteorologiques espagnols. Air Magazine 35. 2007.

Arráez Cerdá, Juan. Los aviones de L´Armeé de l´Air internados en España a la caída de Francia I y II. Historia.

Arráez Cerdá, Juan. Los aviones italianos internados en España durante la Segunda Guerra mundial. Serga nº 47. 2007.

Arráez Cerdá, Juan. Los ingleses también disparan. Vuelos de Ayer.

Aviationcorner.net. Javier González.

Aviationcorner.net. John Mellor.

Aviationcorner.net. Pedro M. Moreno.

Beaman, John R, ; Campbell, Jerry. Messerschmitt Bf 109 in action Part 1. Squadron Signal Publications. 1980

Beaman, John R. Messerschmitt Bf 109 in action Part 2. Squadron Signal Publications. 1983,

Bernard, Denes. Heinkel He 112 in action. Squadron Signal Publications. 1996.

Breffort, Dominique; Jouineau, André. Focke Wulf Fw 190. From 1939 to 1945. Histoire & Collections. 2007.

Breffort, Dominique; Jouineau, André. Messerschmitt Me 109 from 1936 to 1942. Histoire & Collections. 2001.

Breffort, Dominique; Jouineau, André. Messerschmitt Me 109 from 1943 to 1945. Histoire & Collections. 2002.

Bueno Carrera, José María. La División y la Escuadrilla azul. Su organización y uniformes. Aldaba. 2003.

Caballero, Carlos; Guillén, Santiago. Escuadrillas azules en Rusia. Historia y uniformes. Almena. 1999.

Conde Benítez, Manuel. Heinkel He 112 en España, Camuflajes y marcas. Manupedia. 2010.

Caballero Jurado, Carlos. Españoles en la Luftwaffe. Escuadrilla azules en Rusia. Tikal.

Centro de Estudios Borjanos.

De Jong, Peter. Dornier Do 24 Units. Osprey Publishing. 2015.

Díaz Benítez, Juan José. Canarias en la estrategia de EE.UU. durante la II Guerra Mundial y el comienzo de la Guerra Fría. Boletín Millares Carlo. 2010.

Díaz Benítez, Juan José. Canarias en la planificación militar francesa 1941-1943. Boletín Millares Carlo. 2005-2006.

Díaz Benítez, Juan José. La defensa de la Palma durante la Segunda Guerra Mundial. Anuario de estudios atlánticos. 2014.

Díaz Benítez, Juan José. Pilgrim y la defensa de Gran Canaria durante la II Guerra mundial. Anuario de estudios atlánticos. 2000.

Fernández-Coppel Larrinaga, Jorge. La Escuadrilla Azul. La Esfera de los Libros. 2006.

Filley, Brian. Fw 190 in action. Squadron Signal Publications. 1999.

Gil Martínez, Eduardo Manuel. Aeronautica Nazionale Republicana (1943-1945). The Aviation of the Italian Social Republic. Kagero. 2018.

Gil Martínez, Eduardo Manuel. Españoles en las SS y la Wehrmacht 1944-45. La Unidad Ezquerra en la batalla de Berlín. Almena. 2011.

Gil Martínez, Eduardo Manuel. Fuerzas acorazadas húngaras 1939-45. Almena. 2017.

Gil Martínez, Eduardo Manuel. The Spanish in the SS and Wehrmacht 1944-45. The Ezquerra Unit in the Battle of Berlín. Schiffer Publishing.

Gil Martínez, Eduardo Manuel. The Bulgarian Air Force in World War II. Germany´s forgotten Ally. Kagero. 2017.

González Serrano, José Luis. Las unidades y el material del Ejército del Aire durante la Segunda Guerra mundial. AF Editores. 2005.

https://www.facebook.com/notes/antonio-gonz%C3%A1lez-mart%C3%ADnez/los-planes-de-invasi%C3%B3n-de-canarias-en-la-segunda-guerra-mundial-el-plan-pilgrim/10150475236276893/

http://www.forosegundaguerra.com/viewtopic.php?f=15&t=18641&start=45

http://memoriablau.es/viewtopic.php?t=86&start=90

https://www.mve2gm.es

https://ww2aircraft.net/

Ketley, Barry. Luftwaffe emblems. 1939-1945. Crecy Publishing. 2013.

Martínez Canales, Francisco. Alas españolas en Rusia 1941/44. Escuadrillas azules en la Luftwaffe. Almena. 2011.

Mattioli, Marco. Savoia-Marchetti S.79 Sparviero Bomber Units. Osprey Publishing. 2018.

Ministerio de Defensa.

Ministerio de Defensa. Aviones militares españoles.1986.

Modelismo militar e historia/Hobbymodelismo.es

Mollo, A. The armed forces of World War II. Greenwich Editions. 2000.

Murawski, M. Dornier Do17/Do215. Kagero. 2015.

Neulen, Hans Werner. In the skies of Europe. The Crowood Press. 2000.

Peczkowski, Robert. Messerschmitt Bg-109G. Mushroom Model Publications. 2000.

Permuy López, Rafael A. Atlas ilustrado de la aviación en la Guerra Civil Española. Susaeta.

Rodrigo Fernández, Rafael. La defensa de las Islas Baleares durante la primera fase de la Segunda Guerra Mundial. (1939-1940). RUHM 5/Vol 3/2014.

Sáez Rodríguez, Ángel. España ante la Segunda Guerra Mundial. El sistema defensivo contemporáneo del campo de Gibraltar. Historia actual Online. 2011,

Salas Larrazabal, Jesús. La guerra de España desde el aire: Dos ejércitos y sus cazas frente a frente. Ediciones Ariel. 1969.

Servicio Histórico del Ejército del Aire.

Weal, John. Jagdgeschwader 27 "Afrika". Osprey Publishing. 2003.

Weal, John. Jagdgeschwader 51 "Mölders". Osprey Publishing. 2006.

web Españoles en la 2ª Guerra mundial.

www.asisbiz.com

www. Wikipedia.org